Brains
That Work a Little Bit Differently

Brains
That Work a Little Bit Differently

**Recent discoveries about
common mental diversities**

by

Allen D. Bragdon

and

David Gamon, Ph.D.

The
Brainwaves Center
CAPE COD & SAN FRANCISCO

Published by
Brainwaves Books
The Brainwaves Center
Tupelo Road, Bass River, MA 02664-2210
e-mail: brainwaves@mediaone.net

For licensing information or bulk purchases contact
Brainwaves Books at the address above.

The information in this book is intended to provide insight into how the brain functions. It is not intended as an aid to neurological or psychological diagnosis or treatment, all of which must be conducted by qualified practitioners.

Page layout and graphics by Carolyn Zellers. Cover and chapter illustrations by Penny
Neal. Cover design by Cindy Wood. Index by Michael Loo. Admin. by Robert Brogan.

First Edition
Library of Congress Cataloging-in-Publication Data
Bragdon, Allen D.
   Brains that work a little bit differently : recent discoveries about 10 common mental
   diversities / by Allen D. Bragdon and David Gamon. — 1st ed.
      p. cm.
   Includes bibliographical references and index.
   ISBN 0-916410-67-6
      1. Cognition disorders — Popular works. 2. Perception, Disorders of — Popular
works. 3. Left-and right-handedness. 4. Alcoholism. 5. Seasonal affective disorder
— Popular works. 6. Brain — Abnormalities — Popular works. I. Gamon, David.
II. Title.
   RC553.C64B73 2000
   616.8—dc21
                                                                 00-034265

Printed in the United States of America

00 01 02 03   10 9 8 7 6 5 4 3 2 1

EDITOR'S NOTE

The Brainwaves Center undertook to examine the current research into these common diversities because, as a group, they're like the weather. Brain abnormalities affect everyone; human brains are as different as human faces. Yet the causes and consequences of most differences are subtle and complex on the local level; which makes the subject interesting. Diversities such as most of these profoundly torque the private lives of families and the curricula of educational institutions. These clouds burst unexpectedly. The children, especially, are caught without umbrellas.

Why these ten subjects? They are not so rare as to be neurological "cases." With the exception of autism in its severe form these "gentle" abnormalities are found in individuals most of whom live otherwise normal lives. The findings of current science, if understood, bear on their lives by providing insights into symptoms, causes, and correlations with other health matters that statistically accompany each condition. Perhaps some of this new information will empower the empathy of people who want to understand and help others.

We all want to know about whatever marks us as unique without condemning us as freaks. None of the conditions described in this book is typical of the standard blueprint that has evolved for the human brain. Yet, all told, a huge portion of the population of the world lives quietly, often brilliantly, with one or more of these atypical conditions. And others among us sometimes wonder if we too might suffer from one of them, just a little.

— The Editors, The Brainwaves Center

CONTENTS

Contents

ADHD
A Heightened Awareness

Diagnostic Checklist

ADHD is characterized by inattention, hyperactivity, and impulsivity excessive for the age or developmental level. Standard diagnosis specifies that by the time a child reaches seven years, at least six of the features listed below under "inattention," plus a combined total of at least six of the items listed under "hyperactivity" and "impulsivity," must all be present.

1. Inattention:

    (a) won't pay attention to details, makes many careless mistakes in schoolwork or other chores;

    (b) can't sustain attention in tasks or games;

    (c) seems not to listen properly when spoken to;

    (d) doesn't follow instructions well, and often fails to complete tasks;

    (e) has a hard time organizing tasks;

    (f) has a hard time with activities or tasks that require a sustained mental effort;

    (g) frequently loses things needed for tasks or activities, such as pencils, books, toys;

    (h) is easily distracted;

    (i) is often forgetful in routine activities.

2. Hyperactivity:

    (a) fidgets or squirms excessively;

    (b) leaves seat when sitting is required;

    (c) runs around or climbs on things excessively;

    (d) has a hard time with quiet activities;

    (e) seems to be in constant motion;

    (f) talks excessively.

3. Impulsiveness:

    (a) blurts out answers before the question has even been finished;

    (b) has a hard time waiting to take turn;

    (c) interrupts or butts in on others.

Attention-Deficit/ Hyperactivity Disorder

Attention-Deficit/ Hyperactivity Disorder, or ADHD, is one of the most common disorders included in this book. It is generally accepted that about three to five percent of school-age children have it, although some place the rate of occurrence as high as 24 percent. And yet twenty years ago nobody had even heard of the disorder. Have children suddenly become less attentive and more hyperactive?

Probably not. The dramatic increase in ADHD diagnoses is more the result of a heightened awareness of the disorder and the passage of laws requiring public schools to identify and help students who have it. Largely because of this new legislation, outpatient visits for ADHD almost tripled from 1990 to 1993 alone.

The reason, then, that ADHD has become so commonplace is the same reason so many more people suddenly seemed to suffer from low-level depression: behavior that used to be viewed as a sign of weak character is now understood to result from a brain-based imbalance.

In the case of depression, common-enough human feelings such as low self-esteem, pessimism, and passivity are now considered to be linked to low levels of serotonin in the brain, and are treated with drugs of the Prozac class that work by raising levels of that neurotransmitter. By an interesting kind of logic, the very fact that certain temperamental traits can be "cured" on a biochemical level by medication means that people who respond well to such medicine are now understood to be ill, rather than "lazy," or "weak," or "just a little different."

In the case of ADHD, the most widespread current opinion is that this disorder also stems from a neurotransmitter imbalance. According to many researchers, the neurotransmitter implicated in ADHD is dopamine, and something about the brain of someone with ADHD results in dopamine levels being too high. This in turn results in behavior that is, in some ways, the opposite of the dour, stiff, stoic, and eventually physically frozen behavior of someone with a dopamine-deficiency disease like Parkinson's.

One of the reasons the symptoms of ADHD haven't traditionally been taken seriously is that they are, in many ways, exaggerated versions of the kind of behavioral traits that small children typically exhibit anyway — inattentiveness, hyperactivity, and low impulse control. The difference between a child with ADHD and those without it lies in both the severity of the symptoms — especially in children of early school age — and in the delay in outgrowing the inattentive, hyperactive, and impulsive behavior as quickly as other children.

Because children are expected to learn to have more focus and self-control simply in the process of "growing up," older children with ADHD are often treated with disapproval by adults — which only worsens another symptom of ADHD, an acute sense of low self-esteem.

In fact, it makes about as much sense to criticize an ADHD child for being lazy or contrary-minded as it would be to criticize any small child for telling falsehoods in response to the suggestions of an adult. One of the reasons young children's testimony in cases of alleged preschool abuse is viewed so cautiously is that their brains (more specifically, their frontal lobes) simply haven't developed sufficiently to keep careful track of where an idea came from — whether from actual first-hand experience or in response to the suggestion of a well-meaning adult. An understanding of this will help us avoid blaming young children if what they say turns out to be wrong. It's not that they're really lying —it's just that their frontal lobes haven't developed enough to give them the kind of "source memory" that most adults have.

What causes ADHD?
One of the keys to understanding ADHD, as suggested earlier, may lie in the frontal lobes. The front part of the brain houses regions responsible for

ADHD in adults
While many people have heard about ADHD in children, it is also a problem that may affect as much as 2% of the adult population. Adult symptoms include low tolerance for frustration or delay (waiting in line or in traffic can be a major ordeal for ADHD adults), and, in social situations, conduct that could be described as intrusive, gregarious, and over-talkative — the adult version of the class clown. Nonetheless, it is important to remember that ADHD diagnosis in adults is even more difficult to define than it is in children, especially in this caffeine-charged age of digitized information and instant gratification — a time when it seems as if the whole society has a touch of ADHD.

ADHD appears to be a lag or failure in development of at least three areas, primarily in the right side of the brain. These areas dampen and channel requests for action, constantly feeding into the cortex from the more primitive limbic system located in the center of the brain.

"executive-attention" skills — monitoring and regulating one's own behavior, controlling one's emotions, taking the necessary steps to achieve goals, and so on. An imbalance occurs in ADHD between the input of the still immature centers in the right hemisphere (*anterior cingulate*) that focus attention and the prefrontal area that selects goals and predicts how to reach them. (Some research also shows immaturity in another area, near the hearing centers, that coordinates various and varied incoming data into the meaningful "big picture.") Young children, and adults with frontal lobe injury, often lack focus and planning skills, and may seem irresponsible and sometimes even antisocial as a result.

Why would young children lack frontal-lobe-based skills?

To answer this question, it's necessary to correct a common misconception that the quality and quantity of our brain cells are at their peak when we're born, and that things just go downhill from there. In fact, a lot of brain development happens well after birth. The frontal lobes are, in evolutionary terms, the most recently-developed part of our brain. That means that they're also one of the slowest parts to develop as our

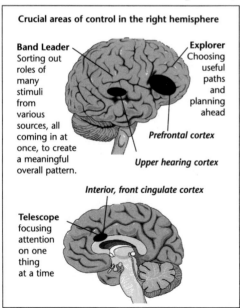

Crucial areas of control in the right hemisphere

Band Leader Sorting out roles of many stimuli from various sources, all coming in at once, to create a meaningful overall pattern.

Explorer Choosing useful paths and planning ahead

Prefrontal cortex

Upper hearing cortex

Interior, front cingulate cortex

Telescope focusing attention on one thing at a time

Working Memory Span

Children with ADHD tend to perform poorly on "executive-control" tasks such as tests of working memory — the kind of short-term memory that allows you to retain information while you're monitoring, judging, or manipulating it "on-line." Amphetamine medication tends to increase attention span and improve working memory tasks.

THE TEST

One test of working memory is called the Working Memory Span. For this test, read each of the three sentences in each set out loud to someone and ask her to tell you immediately after you read each sentence whether it is absurd or makes sense. After each set, ask the person to name the objects (car, sky, etc.) mentioned in the three sentences.

Set 1	Set 2
The mechanic fixed the car.	The boy walked the piano.
The waitress fed the sky.	The teacher graded the test.
The gardener watered the plants.	The man drove the grass.

An Unsettling Discovery

Very recently researchers at the University of Pittsburgh discovered a high correlation between children with lead poisoning (a high level of lead deposits in their bones) and children convicted for legally delinquent behavior. Lead poisoning causes damage to the prefrontal lobes. New research is now under way there to investigate whether a similar correlation exists for children diagnosed as having Attention Deficit Disorder.

brain grows and matures. Some researchers believe that the full development of the brain's frontal cortex isn't complete until the mid-twenties, or even later.

Since the frontal lobes are developing through adolescence even in ADHD children, symptoms of the disorder tend to lessen with age. By early adolescence, a frantic inability to remain seated is often replaced by mere restlessness or fidgetiness, and by early adulthood the fidgetiness may turn into a mere dislike of sedentary activities and a preference for employment and hobbies that permit free and frequent movement. However, symptoms of inattention (for example, difficulty organizing tasks requiring working memory and sustaining effort and attention until completing them) tend not to lessen as much. In about one third of people diagnosed with ADHD in childhood, the symptoms are reduced enough by adolescence that they're no longer considered to have the disorder. The percentage climbs to about 70 by adulthood.

This typical progression of ADHD makes this brain disorder different from many others, such as mood disorders (depression or bipolar disorder, for example) and anxiety disorders. Mood and anxiety disorders may also feature symptoms of inattention but tend to appear only after age seven, and tend to become more severe with age.

What about the role of the neurotransmitter dopamine?

Dopamine is known to be centrally involved in reward-seeking and novelty-seeking behavior, and in the motivation to use and move one's body. As already mentioned, when Parkinson's patients lose the ability to produce dopamine, they become dour, stoic, and, eventually, paralyzed. In many ways, ADHD seems just the opposite of this. So it stands to reason that ADHD symptoms might be related to an excess of dopamine. Support for a role of dopamine in ADHD comes from the seemingly paradoxical success of stimulant drugs (of which Ritalin is one brand name) in alleviating the symptoms of the disorder. The effect of these stimulants seems to be to block the reabsorption of dopamine back into the transmitting brain cell, thereby increasing dopamine levels in the synapse.

The puzzling question this prompts is, if ADHD symptoms result from an *excess* of dopamine, why would *increasing* their levels serve to relieve these symptoms?

Perhaps it isn't really too much dopamine that people with ADHD suffer from. One recent study indicates that ADHD patients actually have an increase in the dopamine *transporter* molecule, which reduces dopamine levels by taking the neurotransmitter back up into the transmitting cell. In that case, though, why is it that ADHD symptoms are essentially the opposite of those of Parkinson's (a dopamine-deficiency disease) and similar to the dopamine-increasing effects of amphetamines?

The answer may lie in findings recently presented by a team of Duke University researchers. By breeding mice lacking the gene for the dopamine transporter ("DAT-knockout" mice), the researchers were able to experiment with animals that showed hyperactive and inattentive behavior that paralleled the behavior of a human with ADHD. The DAT-knockout mice also showed the same paradoxical response to amphetamines as people with ADHD: the treated mice actually calmed down, and performed better on maze-running tests.

Upon close examination of dopamine concentrations in the brains of the DAT-knockout mice, the research team determined that amphetamines that raised dopamine levels in normal mice had no effect on dopamine levels in the DAT-knockout mice. In other words, even though the hyperactive, inattentive behavior of these mice may have been due to excess dopamine, the calming effect of amphetamines couldn't have been due to any effect on dopamine levels, since those levels remained unchanged.

What, then, accounts for the calming effect of amphetamines?
Amphetamines don't just affect dopamine levels, but also raise levels of other neurotransmitters, including serotonin. Serotonin is the neurotransmitter that is raised by drugs such as Prozac. It is considered a "calming" neurotransmitter, conducive to mental focus and well-being. The researchers gave a variety of serotonin-specific drugs to the mice — that is, drugs that raise levels of serotonin but not of any other neurotransmitter — and found that their behavior and learning curves improved just as if they had been given amphetamines. The serotonin-increasing drugs had no effect on the behavior or performance of normal mice. Thus, according to this

evidence, it is a rise in serotonin levels, rather than an increase or decrease in dopamine, that accounts for the beneficial effect of the amphetamines.

A new treatment for ADHD?

These findings have important implications for the treatment of ADHD in humans. Even though children with ADHD have been treated with amphetamines since the 1930s, this kind of treatment has always been controversial. Among other things, there is evidence that amphetamines are "neurotoxic" — harmful to brain cells. If raising serotonin levels relieves ADHD symptoms, then serotonin-selective drugs may be just as helpful in treating these symptoms without any of the harmful side-effects of amphetamines.

Prescribing psychotropic drugs for preschoolers

Parents and teachers well know that the normal behavior of preschoolers often looks a lot like ADHD. A recent survey of state Medicaid programs in the Northwest revealed that the use of stimulants normally prescribed to treat ADHD — most commonly methylphenidate, the generic form of Ritalin — recently increased two- and sometimes threefold for children under four years old. Though such medications are effective for ADHD, an author of that study was doubtful that preschoolers could meet the diagnostic criteria for either ADHD or depression — the probable diagnoses given to justify the prescribed medications.

WHERE TO LEARN MORE:

American Psychiatric Association (1994). Diagnostic and Statistical Manual of Mental Disorders : DSM-IV. Washington, DC: American Psychiatric Association.

Baddeley, A. (1998) "Recent developments in working memory." Current Opinion in Neurobiology 8, 234-238

A. Berger and M.I. Posner (2000). "Pathologies of brain attentional networks." Neuroscience and Biobehavioral Reviews 24: 3-5.

Darin D. Dougherty et al. (1999). "Dopamine transporter density in patients with attention deficit hyperactivity disorder." The Lancet 351: 2132-3.

Editors (2000). "Adult attention deficit hyperactivity disorder." Harvard Health Letter 25/5: 4-5.

Raul R. Gainetdinov et al. (1999). "Role of serotonin in the paradoxical calming effect of psychostimulants on hyperactivity." Science 283: 397-401.

K. Rubia et al. (2000). "Functional frontalisation with age: mapping neurodevelopmental trajectories with fMRI." Neuroscience and Biobehavioral Reviews 24: 13-19.

J.M. Swanson et al. (2000). "Dopamine genes and ADHD." Neuroscience and Biobehavioral Reviews 24: 21-25.

J.M. Swanson et al. (1998). "Attention-deficit hyperactivity disorder and hyperkinetic disorder." The Lancet 351: 429-33.

J.M. Swanson, M. Lerner, and L. Williams (1995). "More frequent diagnosis of attention deficit-hyperactivity disorder." The New England Journal of Medicine 333: 944.

R. Tannock, A. Ickowiz, and R. Schachar (1995). "Differential effects of methylphenidate on working memory in ADHD children with and without comorbid anxiety." Journal of the American Academy of Child and Adolescent Psychiatry 34: 886-96.

Daniela Vallone, Roberto Picetti, and Emiliana Borrelli (2000). "Structure and function of dopamine receptors." Neuroscience and Biobehavioral Reviews 24: 125-32.

Julie Mango Zito et al (2000). "Trends in the prescribing of psychotropic medications to preschoolers." Journal of the American Medical Association 283/8: 1025-30.

ALCOHOLISM, ETC.
Triggering Transmitters

Are You an Alcoholic?

This questionnaire is designed to determine whether your drinking (or that of a friend or family member) is anything to worry about. It is based on a widely used test, called the Michigan Alcohol Screening Test (MAST), by Melvin L. Selzer. (Scoring points are in parentheses.)

1. Do you feel you drink more than others? (2)

2. Have you ever awakened the morning after drinking and found you couldn't remember part of the previous evening? (2)

3. Does a spouse, relative, or close friend ever express concern about your drinking? (1)

4. Do you find it hard to stop after two drinks? (2)

5. Do you ever feel guilty about your drinking? (1)

6. Do friends and relatives think you over-indulge? (2)

7. Are you unable to stop when you want? (2)

8. Have you ever attended a meeting of Alcoholics Anonymous (for yourself)? (5)

9. Have you been in physical fights when drinking? (1)

10. Has your drinking ever created problems between you and a spouse, parent, or other relative? (2)

11. Has your spouse or another family member ever gone to anyone for help about your drinking? (2)

12. Have you ever lost friends due to drinking? (2)

(Continued on page 24)

Reward Deficiency Syndrome?

According to a recent National Center of Addiction and Substance Abuse report, illegal drugs and alcohol are responsible for the imprisonment of 80 percent of the inmates currently serving time in American prisons. This includes inmates who stole to support their habits, broke drug- and alcohol-related laws, or broke other laws while under the influence. And yet relatively few correctional institution resources are devoted to drug or alcohol treatment programs, let alone to solving the problem of addiction at the level of brain biochemistry. That's one reason for the high recidivism rates, and why so many just-released prisoners will soon return to jail.

The National Institute on Drug Abuse estimates that about four million Americans are addicted to illicit drugs, and that about 14 million are alcoholics. At first glance this would not appear to be a difficult concept to come to grips with, but a quick look at the diagnostic questionnaire at the beginning of this section will show you that alcoholism can be a very slippery subject and quite difficult to define. Some of the criteria have to do with social attitudes ("Does a spouse, relative, or close friend ever express concern about your drinking?") that may shift from one culture or generation to another. Other questions ("Have you ever neglected your obligations, your family, or your work for two or more days because you were drinking?") refer to the potential of alcohol to interfere with desirable goals in the life of the user.

The standard desk reference "Diagnostic and

(Continued from page 22)

13. Have you ever gotten into trouble at work or school because of drinking? (2)

14. Have you ever lost a job because of drinking? (2)

15. Have you ever neglected your obligations, family, or work for two days because you were drinking? (2)

16. Do you drink before noon fairly often? (1)

17. Have you ever been told you have liver trouble? (2)

18. After having been drinking, have you ever had delirium tremens ("the DTs"), or severe shaking? (5)

19. Have you ever gone to anyone for help about your drinking? (5)

20. Have you ever been in a hospital because of drinking? (5)

21. Have you ever been a patient in a psychiatric hospital where drinking was part of the problem that resulted in hospitalization? (2)

22. Have you ever been seen at a psychiatric or mental health clinic or gone to any doctor, social worker or clergyman for help with any emotional issues where drinking was part of the problem? (2)

23. Have you ever been arrested for driving under the influence? (2 pts. each time)

24. Have you ever been arrested or taken into custody because of drunken behavior? (2 each time)

Scoring:

5 points or more: You are an alcoholic.

4 points.: You may be an alcoholic.

3 points or fewer: You are not an alcoholic.

Statistical Manual of Mental Disorders" (DSM-IV) divides what it calls *Alcohol Use Disorders* into precisely defined subcategories. One is *Alcohol Abuse,* which refers to the extent that the misuse of alcohol interferes with the duties of work, school, and personal life. Diminished job productivity due to hangovers can be a sign of alcohol abuse; so can getting fired due to drinking. Driving while legally drunk, as well as incurring the legal consequences of such behavior, are signs of alcohol abuse, as are alcohol-related quarrels and acts of domestic violence, especially if the drinker continues his alcohol consumption in spite of an awareness of the link between drinking and destructive behavior.

Another subcategory is *Alcohol Dependence,* which refers to a state in which the user either has evidence of tolerance to alcohol, or experiences symptoms of withdrawal upon ceasing to drink. Withdrawal symptoms can run the gamut from anxiety or hand tremors all the way to epileptic-like grand mal seizures. Tolerance for alcohol is likewise a relative concept, but it is sometimes defined in terms of a certain level of alcohol in the body (100 mg. of ethanol — alcohol's active ingredient — per deciliter of blood) with no signs of intoxication.

Some prominent addiction experts point out that, for drugs in general, a definition of addiction in terms of physical withdrawal symptoms is outdated. Some people with alcohol dependence never show any physical symptoms upon withdrawal, and some of the most addictive drugs — cocaine, for example — trigger few physical withdrawal symptoms. But there is one criterion that few would argue with. The crucial feature of addiction — indeed, its very essence, according to the National Institute on Drug Abuse — lies in "compulsive drug seeking and use, even in the face of negative health and social consequences." It is this out-of-control, self-destructive characteristic of alcoholism and other drug addictions that truly reflects their status as disorders of the brain.

Is alcoholism a brain disorder?

The more we understand about what's going on in the brain of a person addicted to alcohol, nicotine, or illicit drugs, the harder it is to view addicts as simply weak-willed, or self-indulgent. In fact, in the view of a great many researchers, the only rational approach to the problem of addiction is to treat it as a chronic brain disease — perhaps not curable, but certainly manageable.

It is now clear there are two ways that addiction can be viewed as a disorder of the brain. First, research from a variety of angles converges on the idea that certain innate brain differences predispose some people to addiction more than others. Second, once someone starts abusing alcohol, cocaine, heroin or amphetamines, long-term alteration of brain structure and function make it extremely difficult to abstain from the addictive drug by will power alone.

Some of the evidence for the role of genetic factors in alcoholism comes from studies of twins. Among genetically identical twins, if one twin is alcoholic the risk of the second also being alcoholic is significantly higher than among fraternal, non-identical twins. And if children of someone with alcohol dependence are adopted by non-alcoholics, their risk for developing alcoholism is three to four times higher than in children of non-alcoholic parents. This same increased risk factor also applies in more general situations: if you have a close relative who is an alcoholic, your chances of developing alcohol dependence is three to four times higher than if you don't. So alcoholism is not only a result of the environment one grows up in, or a matter of "strength of character," but a consequence of the genes one inherits.

Further evidence that alcoholism is, in part, genetically determined comes from animal studies. Many researchers have found that they can influence alcohol drinking behavior in rodents by selectively breeding them for certain genetic traits. One recent study provides evidence that a genetic predisposition towards alcoholism may lie in individual differences in the brain's *opioid system* — the part of the brain that responds to pleasure-inducing molecules such as enkephalins and endorphins.

Mice and monkeys that are given a drug that blocks opioid receptors — that is, makes it impossible for certain brain cells to respond to opioids — show little interest in "drinking" compared to other mice and monkeys. In the recent study just mentioned, the researchers selected one group of rats bred for strong alcohol preference and another group bred to show no fondness for alcohol. In the group of "drinkers," parts of the brain responsive to a given dose of alcohol turned out to produce a significantly greater quantity of opioids than in the group of nondrinkers. It may therefore be that people who naturally have an opioid system that is strongly responsive to alcohol are more likely to enjoy and crave alcohol, and more likely to become alcoholics.

Other very recent work has implicated the neurotransmitter gamma-aminobutyric acid (GABA) in alcohol's alluring, and addictive, effect on the brain. According to a University of North Carolina study, brain chemicals called *neurosteroids* are released in response to ethanol, the active ingredient in alcohol. Neurosteroids appear to strengthen the effect of chemicals that act on GABA receptors, including ethanol. One of the roles of GABA, and the receptors it acts on, is to inhibit the brain and body's stress response.

This suggests the possibility that one risk factor for alcoholism may be a low level of neurosteroids in the brain, which would predispose a person to dependence on alcohol to achieve a normal "relaxation" response to stress. Women naturally produce higher levels of neurosteroids than men, and men have higher rates of alcoholism. Also, women's neurosteroid levels fluctuate across their menstrual cycle, so women may be more vulnerable to alcohol's appeal during some parts of the cycle than during others.

Even though different addictive drugs trigger different brain chemicals — opioids and the neurotransmitters serotonin and GABA, for example — some researchers maintain that all drugs of abuse share a common mechanism that activates our brain's "pleasure circuit." The brain evolved this reward system to

The brain's desire-action-reward loop

The brain has evolved to provide rewards so the body will invest its energy in taking action to meet an essential survival need. Going out to find food and eating it when you feel hunger is an example. This system works for all survival needs from sex to defecation, and it faithfully keeps on working even when masked drugs break into the cycle to plunder its reward-and-satisfaction phases.

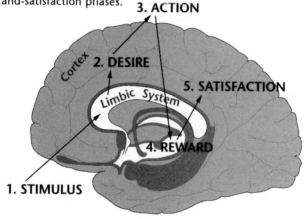

(1) News of a STIMULUS, stress for example, reaches the *Limbic System* (relatively primitive functions in the center of the brain). The *Cortex* (higher functions with conscious thought) registers a **(2)** DESIRE and takes **(3)** ACTION by drinking alcohol, for example. This causes the *Limbic System* to generate a **(4)** REWARD, dopamine for example, which **(5)** registers in the *Cortex* as SATISFACTION of the original desire.

motivate organisms to seek food (keyed to the amount of glucose in the blood) and other requirements for survival when needed. This loop of "desire" to "action" to "reward" (in humans, the release of dopamine) also works for addictions such as alcoholism. The crucial mechanism, according to the director of the National Institute on Drug Abuse, is the neurotransmitter dopamine, and all drugs of pleasure work by raising its levels in the brain. Cocaine and amphetamines, for example, do this by interfering with a molecule that pulls dopamine back out of the synapse — the communication point between brain cells — after it has been released by the transmitting cell. The result is higher levels of dopamine overall.

The way that the brain responds to this increase in dopamine levels is initially, of course, to feel good. But eventually, chronic drug use harms the brain's natural ability to produce dopamine and even kills some of the brain's dopamine receptors. That means the user has to go back to the drug just in order to try and regain normal dopamine levels.

This kind of brain response is the second way that addiction really is like a brain disorder. An addicted brain is one that has been altered by a drug to the degree that it is no longer in command of its own normal operation. That, in a nutshell, is addiction.

While all addictive drugs trick the brain into producing a normal level of dopamine, there's also increasing evidence that dopamine isn't the whole story. We've already considered the argument for the role of opioids like endorphin in the pleasurable effect of alcohol. For cocaine, there's compelling evidence that the neurotransmitter serotonin's role is crucial.

This evidence comes from experiments with "knockout" rodents. These laboratory mice or rats are not unusually beautiful, they have been selectively bred to lack a gene that affects behavior by modifying specific brain structures. One recent experiment involved rodents in which the dopamine transporter (DAT) was knocked out. DAT acts like a janitor. It picks up and carries away the neurotransmitter dopamine out of the synapse after the dopamine has done its job. As a result, those mice have higher levels of dopamine. This activates the receptors on that neuron more powerfully which, in turn, normally creates a feeling of pleasure. Since cocaine interferes with the clean-up function of DAT in normal mice (as well as in humans) why would mice that had their DAT gene knocked out in the first place continue to show interest in cocaine? If cocaine can't possibly raise their dopamine levels any further, those mice should have no reason to feel the pleasurable affects of cocaine.

In fact, the mice in this experiment continued to self-administer cocaine, even in preference to eating. Analysis of their brains revealed activation of systems triggered by a *different* neurotransmitter called *serotonin* (the same neurotransmitter that antidepressants like Prozac elevate). That is why, in fact, it may be serotonin that is at least partly responsible for the pleasurable effect of cocaine which leads to addiction.

Treatment

Alcohol dependence is a complex disease that most public health policy experts agree requires a complex treatment response. One challenge in dealing with drug addiction of any kind is that so many things can trigger drug cravings in addition to the aspects of brain chemistry we've just considered. For one thing, intensely pleasurable drug-induced experiences can permanently lodge themselves in the brain as "emotional memories," even if other drug-related systems in an ex-drug abuser's brain have been successfully

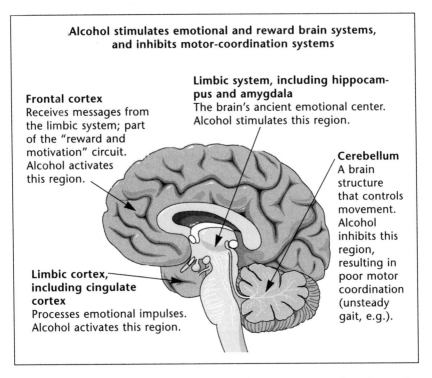

Alcohol stimulates emotional and reward brain systems, and inhibits motor-coordination systems

Frontal cortex
Receives messages from the limbic system; part of the "reward and motivation" circuit. Alcohol activates this region.

Limbic system, including hippocampus and amygdala
The brain's ancient emotional center. Alcohol stimulates this region.

Cerebellum
A brain structure that controls movement. Alcohol inhibits this region, resulting in poor motor coordination (unsteady gait, e.g.).

Limbic cortex, including cingulate cortex
Processes emotional impulses. Alcohol activates this region.

treated. These emotional memories may be triggered at any time, but are especially likely if the former addict finds himself in a situation — in a certain place or among certain people — associated with memories of using the drug. So in addition to pharmaceuticals that interact with brain chemistry, these other social-context factors must be also considered.

As for pharmaceuticals, many researchers are working on developing drugs that will somehow counteract the brain responses that lead to enjoyment and abuse of addictive drugs, and to cravings for them. A medication called *buproprion,* sold under the name Zyban, has been effective in helping smokers to quit, perhaps because it raises level of neurotransmitters (dopamine and epinephrine) that smokers otherwise rely on nicotine to raise.

For alcoholism, one pharmaceutical that is currently being tested is *naltrexone*. Naltrexone is an opioid antagonist, interacting with the brain's opioid "reward" system to reduce alcohol cravings. Thus far, the drug has shown some initial effectiveness in reducing relapse rates among recovering alcoholics.

The challenge in designing drugs to combat addiction will be to refine them so that they affect only the brain systems causing the addiction. A drug that shuts down the entire dopamine or opioid "pleasure circuit," for example, would nullify all the beneficial effects of those systems in reinforcing healthy reward- and goal-directed behavior. As the tools available to researchers become increasingly precise so does their ability to trace the precise ways addictive drugs act on the brain. Consequently, the prospects are improving that addicts will be able to regain and retain control of their own brains in the future.

WHERE TO LEARN MORE:

American Psychiatric Association (1994). Diagnostic and Statistical Manual of Mental Disorders: DSM-IV. Washington, DC: American Psychiatric Association.

Kenneth Blum et al. (1996). "Reward deficiency syndrome." American Scientist 84.

S. Barak Caine (1998). "Cocaine abuse: hard knocks for the dopamine hypothesis?" Nature Neuroscience 1/2: 90-92.

A.M. Catafau et al. (1999). "Regional cerebral blood flow changes in chronic alcoholic patients induced by naltrexone challenge during detoxification." Journal of Nuclear Medicine 40/1: 19-24.

M. Ingvar et al. (1998). "Alcohol activates the cerebral reward system in man." Journal of Studies on Alcohol 59/3: 258-69.

Alan I. Leshner (1997). "Addiction is a brain disease, and it matters." Science 278: 45-7.

A. Leslie Morrow et al. (1999). "Neurosteroids mediate pharmacological effects of ethanol: a new mechanism of ethanol action?" Alcohol: Clinical and Experimental Research 23/12: 1933-9.

Beatriz A. Rocha et al. (1998). "Cocaine self-administration in dopamine-transporter knockout mice." Nature Neuroscience 1/2: 132-7.

M.J. VanDoren et al. (2000). "Neuroactive steroid 3a-hydroxy-5a-pregnan-20-one modulates electro-physiological and behavioral actions of ethanol." Journal of Neuroscience 20/5: 1982-89.

Francis J. White (1998). "Cocaine and the serotonin saga." Nature 393: 118-19.

Christopher S. Wren (1998). "Drugs or alcohol linked to 80% of inmates." New York Times January 9, 1998: 14.

AUTISM
A Mind Unaware of Itself and Others

Diagnosing Autism

The standard diagnostic manual of mental illness, the DSM-IV, specifies several clusters of criteria for an autism diagnosis. The following list applies to Autistic Disorder, the relatively well-defined center of the category of autistic-like conditions:

1. **Impairment in social interaction:**
   (a) impairment in nonverbal communication, such as eye-to-eye contact, body postures, and hand gestures;
   (b) failure to develop age-appropriate friendships;
   (c) lack of interest in sharing achievements or enjoyment with others.

2. **Impairment in communication:**
   (a) delay in speech development, or lack of spoken language development;
   (b) decisive impairment in maintaining a conversation;
   (c) repetitive use of words or phrases;
   (d) lack of spontaneous make-believe play.

3. **Repetitive patterns of behavior, interests, and activities:**
   (a) intense, focused preoccupation with a single interest;
   (b) inflexible adherence to specific rituals or habits;
   (c) repetitive body movements (e.g., rocking);
   (d) preoccupation with parts of objects.

A Bit of Raymond Babbit's World

Anyone who saw Dustin Hoffman's portrayal of Raymond Babbitt in the movie *Rain Man* came away with a vivid image of autism: the social strangeness, the weird tics and repetitive rituals, the below-average IQ combined with a phenomenal ability in one specific area. But Raymond Babbitt's kind of autism is just one example of a range of disorders so broad that nobody knows just how many people should be called autistic.

The statistics that are usually stated suggest that autism occurs in between two and five children out of 10,000, at a ratio of four or five boys to one girl. But in addition to "classic" autism, as first described by Leo Kanner in 1943, there are many other disorders, such as Asperger syndrome (sometimes considered a kind of "high-functioning autism," lacking the language problems of "classic" autism) and anorexia nervosa, that either overlap with autism or mark the fuzzy edges of the category. Autism can be accompanied by severe mental retardation, somewhat low IQ, or normal IQ. Only in a minority of cases does autism go hand-in-hand with Raymond Babbitt's type of prodigious ability.

Even in cases of the kind of "classic" autism that pinpoints the center of the category, the disorder is considered a *syndrome* — a cluster of features that tend to "go together" (the literal meaning of *syndrome* in Greek) — but that probably can't be tied to a single underlying cause. This makes it different from — and harder to pin down, diagnose, and treat than — a discrete problem such as asthma.

Diagnosing "classic" autism

The undisputed center of the autism category is occupied by Autistic Disorder, also known as Kanner autism, childhood autism, or early infantile autism. The essential features of Autistic Disorder must be present by age three, hence the terms "early infantile" or "childhood."

The most salient symptom of Autistic Disorder is impaired social interaction and communication. In an infant, this can show itself in a dislike of cuddling and physical affection, avoidance of eye contact, and lack of response to parents' voices. Later on, the child will show little interest in making friends, participating in ordinary, everyday activities, or sharing achievements, such as exhibiting the pride children often display following the unexpected discovery of a sea shell or brightly-colored pebble. In fact, it is not uncommon for autistic children to appear completely oblivious to another child's distress, or even to the mere presence of other children at all.

Autistic children may also experience delay in developing language skills. In some cases spoken language may never develop. If and when it does, their speech will often exhibit unusual intonation and rhythm, and include repetitive words and phrases. Even when they seem to have achieved an adequate grasp of vocabulary and grammatical structures, autistic children typically experience difficulties in the kind of conversation that would be normal for their age.

Another autistic feature — and one that is often the most obvious to the casual observer of an older child — is a preoccupation with repetitive patterns of behavior that run the gamut from unusual mannerisms, such as rocking back and forth or the flapping of hands, to an obsessive interest in a narrow domain of facts, such as license plate numbers or baseball statistics. Closely related to this is the autistic's fear of change on even the most trivial level, such as taking a new and different route to school.

Autism as a faulty "theory of mind"

Unfortunately, a simple list of the diagnostic symptoms exhibited by autistic individuals doesn't tell us much about the underlying problems. However, one recent insight into the puzzle that lends a measure of understanding to the many diverse symptoms of the disorder is that autism may be the failure to develop a normal "theory of mind."

Typically, children learn to see the world from the perspective of others — a skill called *empathy*. By the age of four, most children are capable of making what are known as *first-order belief attributions*, such as: "I think that he thinks that...." By age seven, they've moved on to second-order belief attributions, such as: "I think that he thinks that she thinks that...."

If a child with Autistic Disorder ever develops even the first-order belief attribution skills, it won't be until adolescence. Even as adults, second-order belief attribution is totally lacking. This lack of a "theory of mind" also explains why people with autism appear

Testing theories of mind: the strange stories test

Autism researcher F. Happé devised a "strange stories test" to determine people's ability to attribute the right attitude to another person from what they do or say. In this test, people with autism can figure out that what Sarah says isn't true, but not that she's being sarcastic.

Jimmy has invited Sarah to a restaurant for her birthday. He tells her that the restaurant he chose, Le Français, *has excellent French food and great service — probably better than any restaurant she's ever eaten in. When they get there, the waiter is rude, the wine is sour, and the soufflé is cold. Sarah says, "Oh, sure, this is a great place you took me for my birthday."*

Is it true, what Sarah says?

Why does she say it?

If you give this test to normal adults, most of them might tell you that Sarah's remark is a sarcastic comment in response to her irritation that her friend took her to such a bad restaurant on her birthday, after he had claimed it would be such a wonderful treat for her. An autistic adult, on the other hand, will be more likely to say that Sarah's remark is, say, a "white lie" intended to make her friend feel better after the disappointing experience. In other words, someone with autism will be able to recognize that a remark isn't true, but won't understand the other person's attitude behind the remark.

to show so little compassion for others, yet have such difficulty in deceiving others. Psychopaths, by contrast, combine lack of compassion with excellent deception skills — it's their *emotional* capacity for *sympathy* that malfunctions, not their *cognitive* capacity for *empathy*.

Some researchers feel that once autism is viewed in these terms, it can then be best understood as merely one of many other clusters of empathy disorders that are known by different names and exhibit different forms of superficial expression. For example, *anorexia nervosa* — an eating disorder most common among girls and women — which typically involves extreme obsessiveness, limited social interaction, and limited ability to speak about feelings, may be a "female" expression of the more typically male, classic Autistic Disorder.

Can autistic children lead normal lives as adults?
The prognosis for autistic children growing up to be able to lead a "normal" life in adulthood varies according to the individual's level of general intelligence and language development. For autistic children with severe mental retardation, the prognosis is poor. Among adults with autism, about one-third achieve partial independence, living, for example, in a half-way house and performing closely supervised work. A small percentage of the highest-functioning autistic adults live complete independent lives but their limited social interaction and communication skills, and their narrow range of interests and activities, might still cause them to be considered "odd."

What causes autism?

The only thing everyone can agree upon is that no single brain abnormality exists that can sufficiently explain autism or what causes it. For decades after Leo Kanner wrote about the disorder, autism was actually believed to have a psychological basis — the result of "cold," uncaring parents, for example — rather than an organic one.

It is now generally believed that the disorder can lay claim to a genetic contribution, as it is often accompanied by problems such as fragile X syndrome — an inherited genetic condition associated with mental retardation. But even among identical twins, one may be autistic while the other is not. So the consensus is that, while genetic factors may play a role, they aren't sufficient to guarantee the development of autism. And while many structural and functional abnormalities have been found in the brains of autistic people, the only universally accepted finding is that no single brain abnormality is present in all cases.

Some brain-imaging studies have shown hemispheric abnormalities among autistic individuals — usually that the left hemisphere is not as active as in a "normal" brain. With most people, the left hemisphere receives more blood than the right, even when the brain is at rest, but

When the brain is "resting," the left side normally receives more blood than the right; in some people with autism, on the other hand, flow is equal.

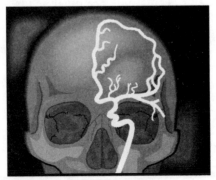

some people with autism have equal at-rest blood flow in both left and right hemispheres. It has also been observed that areas of an autistic brain that receive a relatively low blood flow as compared with that of a normal brain include regions that deal with language and analytical skills. The poor development of language and analytical abilities characteristic of autism, then, may be associated with an underactive left hemisphere. The right hemisphere, on the other hand — the seat of visual and musical skills that aren't affected by autism — is no less active in autistic brains than in normal ones.

Other recent functional imaging analyses have shown that normal people, when performing a "theory of mind" task, show activity in a very specific part of the left prefrontal cortex. People with Asperger syndrome (an autism-like disorder) show activity in an adjacent area, but not in the location usually associated with this kind of reasoning task.

Other studies have found that some autistic persons have abnormalities in the cerebellum, a structure that wraps around the brain stem and, among its other activities, helps regulate motor movements and body posture. Abnormalities in the limbic system involving structures responsible for emotion, memory, and learning have also been found. Since these kinds of behavior and ability are ones that make autistic people seem different from "normal" people, it makes sense that these structural brain abnormalities might play a role in the autistic syndrome. But what causes the abnormalities in the first place — oxygen-deprivation before or during birth in combination with a

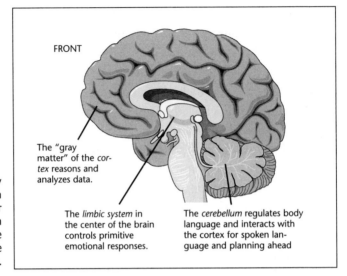

FRONT

The "gray matter" of the *cortex* reasons and analyzes data.

The *limbic system* in the center of the brain controls primitive emotional responses.

The *cerebellum* regulates body language and interacts with the cortex for spoken language and planning ahead

Cutaway view down the center of the brain leaving the right side visible.

genetic predisposition, or what have you — remains a topic of investigation.

People with autism aren't merely "deficient"

Even though autism is considered a disability, it isn't as clear a deficiency as is, say, severe mental retardation. For one thing, some studies show that on tests of certain visual skills, people with autism do better than average. And then there are the autistic savants of the Raymond Babbitt kind — the ones who, in extreme cases, can't add or subtract but can reel off ten-digit prime numbers, or tell you the day of the week of any date within the last 40,000 years, as easily as you could multiply 12 by 12 in your head.

One feature many autistic savants share is the sense that numbers, or whatever the material of their special skill, are their "friends" — perhaps the best or only friends they'll ever have. This close and personal attachment to their special skill, such as numerical calculations or music, becomes a rich and meaningful relationship rather than a purely intellectual or abstract association. Geniuses often seem to have this same sort of attitude towards their domain of expertise. As the mathematical genius Alexander Craig Aitken put it in his description of his associations with the number 7:

> The line of poetry "They passed the pleiades and the planets seven" — mysteries in the minds of the ancients — Sabbath or the seventh day — religious observance of Sunday — 7 in contrast with 13 and 3 in superstition — 7 as a recurring decimal .1402857 which, multiplied by 123456, gives the same numbers in cyclic order — a poem on numbers by Binyon, seen in a review lately — I could quote from it.

The poor social skills and the social isolation characteristic of autism may in fact encourage autistics to live within and explore their private world more than they otherwise would. Indeed, the downside of pushing autistic savants into a more social lifestyle is that they may lose their special skill and thus much of the meaning they find in life.

 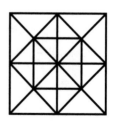

Does the complex figure on the right contain the simpler one at left? If you can see where it is, color it in. People with autism perform better than average on some visual skills tests like picking out the embedded figure in this task.

Another talent autistic savants often share with more "run-of-the-mill" geniuses is that both have the ability to grasp concepts instantaneously, and independently of the medium of language; that, for example, 3,727 is or is not a prime number, or that a given tone is or isn't a perfect B-sharp. Again, consider Alexander Aitken's description of his own thought process in multiplying 123 by 456:

> I do this in two moves: I see at once that 123 times 45 is 5535 and that 123 times 6 is 738; I hardly have to think. Then 55350 plus 738 gives 56088. Even at the moment of registering 56088, I have checked it by dividing by 8, so 7011, and this by 9, 779. I recognize 779 as 41 by 19; and 41 by 3 is 123, 19 by 24 is 456. A check you see; and it passes by in about one second.

Unlike Aitken, autistic savants do not have the ability to articulate their thought processes in performing their feats, but a great deal of evidence points to a reliance on an unusual kind of visual memory. A pair of idiot savant identical twins described by neurologist Oliver Sacks could readily repeat back a 300-digit number, or deduce 20-digit prime numbers in their heads. "Deduce" may not be quite the right word here, since they didn't seem to rely on any kind of calculation — in fact no straightforward algorithm exists for identifying large primes — but on something more like an ability to "see" certain kinds of number or number sequences. Indeed, with their IQ of 60, these twins couldn't even add or subtract accurately.

Again, the theory that some facets of the autistic syndrome may rely on the brain's right hemisphere, and on visual brain systems, rather than on more typical left-brain-based analytical and verbal processing, seems to apply. According to some theorists, autistic savants — and savants in general — lack (as researchers Dieci and Guarnieri put it) "the ability to process complex information at a high level and to store data in an integrated way." Assuming that this inability stems from damage to the brain regions that would normally handle such information-processing tasks, autistic savants fall back on other, more primitive but also more narrowly focused brain regions, allowing them to "understand some simple problems in their essence, free from the load of associations that a normal intelligence automatically creates."

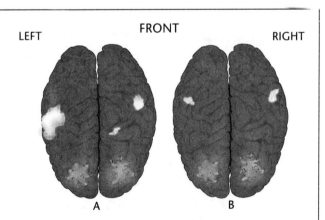

LEFT   FRONT   RIGHT

A   B

These illustrations, based on PET scan images, show a normal brain (A) and an autistic brain (B) while performing language-processing tasks. In the normal brain, left-hemisphere language regions (large white area) are strongly activated. In the autistic brain, left-side language regions show relatively little activity.

WHERE TO LEARN MORE:

American Psychiatric Association (1994). Diagnostic and Statistical Manual of Mental Disorders: DSM-IV. Washington, DC: American Psychiatric Association.

A. Bailey et al. (1998). "A clinicopathological study of autism." Brain 121: 889-995.

C. Chiron et al. (1995). "SPECT of the brain in childhood autism: evidence for a lack of normal hemispheric asymmetry." Developmental Medicine and Child Neurology 37: 849-60.

Shoumitro Deb and Bill Thompson (1998). "Neuroimaging in autism." British Journal of Psychiatry 173: 299-302.

Massimiliano Dieci and A. Monti Guarnieri (1990). "The idiot savant: a reconsideration of the syndrome." American Journal of Psychiatry 147/10: 1387-8.

Christopher L. Gillberg (1992). "The Emanuel Miller Memorial Lecture 1991. Autism and autistic-like conditions: subclasses among disorders of empathy." Journal of Child Psychology and Psychiatry 33/5: 813-42.

F. Happé et al. (1996). "'Theory of mind' in the brain. Evidence from a PET scan study of Asperger syndrome." Neuroreport 8/1: 197-201.

Therese Jolliffe and Simon Baron-Cohen (1999). "The Strange Stories Test: a replication with high-functioning adults with autism or Asperger syndrome." Journal of Autism and Developmental Disorders 29/5: 395-406.

Linda J. Lotspeich and Roland D. Ciaranello (1993). "The neurobiology and genetics of infantile autism." International Review of Neurobiology 35: 87-129.

Howard A. Ring at al. (1999). "Cerebral correlates of preserved cognitive skills in autism: a functional MRI study of Embedded Figures Task performance." Brain 122: 1305-15.

Oliver Sacks (1985). "The twins." The New York Review of Books, February 28 1985: 16-20.

Jeremy D. Schmahmann and Janet C. Sherman (1998). "The cerebellar cognitive affect syndrome." Brain 121: 561-79.

Darold A. Treffert (1988). "The idiot savant: a review of the syndrome." American Journal of Psychiatry 145: 563-72.

DÉJÀ VU
True Hallucinations

CASE HISTORIES

Temporal Lobe Epilepsy and Déjà Vu

People with major temporal lobe epilepsy experience a characteristic "aura" before they lose consciousness. The aura is a cluster of feelings and sensations including a sensation of déjà vu. A variety of patients tell what they feel as the seizure starts in the temporal lobe of their brains. (See page 55.)

■ *Things are deformed; I talk faster; I stammer; I am another person and I seem to be elsewhere; I see again things, scenes; I can lose my body; when I look at myself in the mirror, my face is deformed.*

■ *The impression of having already done what I am in the process of doing; it seems to me that I have already lived through the entire situation; with a feeling of strangeness and also of fear.*

■ *A sensation of being projected into the past coupled with a feeling of having already lived through the present situation.*

■ *Faraway-seeming, muffled auditory illusions.*

■ *A rising sensation from the stomach, fear, a sense of having had "a seizure in the same place, of having felt there the same anxiety."*

■ *A sense of detachment, of being surrounded by a vast emptiness, of undulation, fear, auditory illusions of rhythmic, halting voices, muffled as if spoken from behind a handkerchief.*

■ *A sensation of vertigo and of reliving an already-lived scene; a bitter taste.*

■ *Some object would suddenly seem somehow "magnificent" and "pleasurable"; a bitter taste.*

A MOMENTARY MADNESS

There are certain run-of-the-mill experiences that give all of us a little taste of what it might be like to be insane or to have a brain disorder. Dreams, for example, are sometimes viewed by poets as allowing us nightly access into the mind of a madman. *Déjà vu* (literally, "already seen") is the common term for a familiar experience that is nevertheless bizarre — a brief but overwhelming sense of having already lived through the present moment, and of being able to predict what is about to happen next.

That uncanny feeling may stem from what some psychologists and neurologists call a *doubling of consciousness*. All such experiences share these three characteristics: 1) simultaneous sensations of familiarity and strangeness, 2) a conviction of having experienced something before and yet, 3) an understanding that, realistically, it is impossible to have had that experience. As such, déjà vu is one of a class of experiences that make us aware that our brains are less seamlessly unified than we sometimes assume.

Variations on the same theme
Déjà vu can also be grouped with a variety of memory distortions known as *paramnesia*. Other types of paramnesia include:

False memory — the inclusion of false details in the recollection of past events. False memory problems are common, and they don't usually result in any harm. A notable exception is in court cases, where someone's life or liberty may hinge on a witness's testimony. Serious research into the reliability of eyewitness reports has led to the conclusion that human memory is highly malleable. Memory is not like a passive video recorder that simply plays the event back in its originally witnessed form. Instead, naturally occurring mechanisms in the human brain actively attempt to reconstruct something that has happened in the past. In doing so, it often unconsciously fills in details of what *should* have taken place based on other past experiences.

Confabulation — the unconscious fabrication of patently wrong memories. For example, when asked what she did the previous night, a bedridden woman suffering from confabulation may claim to have run many miles to deliver stolen documents to a foreign government agent. Confabulation may result from frontal lobe injury or organic brain disease, such as Alzheimer's, or from a mental illness such as schizophrenia.

Jamais vu (literally "never seen") — a false sensation that a familiar situation or experience is strangely unfamiliar. Jamais vu can be associated with epilepsy or schizophrenia.

Déjà vu is essentially the opposite of jamais vu, although déjà vu is more common in a healthy brain. Déjà vu can, however, be a sign of a more serious problem, just as confabulation and jamais vu can be.

The harmless, run-of-the-mill type of déjà vu is sometimes called a "minor form" of the phenomenon. This variety appears and disappears rapidly, and does not seriously interfere with the perception of reality. In other words, this kind of déjà vu experience isn't actually confused with a real memory.

In the variety of déjà vu called the "major form," the eerie sensation of having already lived through a novel experience lasts longer, and may be permanently incorporated into a new, false version of reality. The major form of déjà vu can be a symptom of schizophrenia, a mood disorder such as bipolar disorder (manic depression), or an organic brain disorder such as temporal lobe epilepsy. (See page 50 for descriptions in their own words by subjects who suffer from it.)

What causes déjà vu? — many theories, few facts
Even though déjà vu is an experience familiar to most people, few people have any idea what causes it, or what its significance is. That isn't to say that theorists from various professions haven't come up with imaginative, often quite fanciful, interpretations. Parapsychologists have proposed that déjà vu is a "sentiment of pre-existence" resulting from reincarnation, or that it derives from telepathy or astral projection. Freud speculated in *The Interpretation of Dreams* that a déjà vu experience in a dream symbolizes "the genitals of the dreamer's mother; there is indeed no other place about which one can assert with such conviction that one has been there before."

Perhaps it is a matter of timing

A theory that is somewhat easier to take seriously proposes an explanation in terms of a timing problem between the brain's left and right hemispheres. Each hemisphere perceives events and records information independently of the other, but constant instantaneous communication between the brain's two sides gives us the illusion of unity. If, however, there is a brief delay in transmission from the "non-dominant" (usually right) to the "dominant" (usually left) hemisphere, the dominant side receives the same information twice, once directly and once after a brief delay from the opposite half of the brain. This amounts to a kind of mental *diplopia* (literally "double vision"). It is like listening simultaneously to two broadcasts of, say, the same political debate, one of which has a half-second broadcasting delay relative to the other.

Did you dream it once, long ago?

Some psychologists have attributed déjà vu to a memory of a dream. By this theory, a hitherto unrecollected dream is recalled at the precise moment that a waking experience occurs that matches enough of the particulars of the dream. But since the person in the midst of déjà vu fails to realize that an unconscious prior dream is triggering the sensation of familiarity, the recollection appears strangely and mysteriously real.

This theory is of limited use, of course, because it is speculative and untestable. However, there is some intriguing evidence of a connection between dreams and déjà vu. In a study of 58 of his patients, one psychotherapist found that the ten of them who claimed not to dream also claimed never to have had a déjà vu experience.

Is too little or too much déjà vu a bad sign?
According to questionnaire-based surveys, 96 percent of the respondents say they have experienced déjà vu. There is some evidence that the frequency naturally tapers off as people move from childhood into adulthood. If it's true that non-dreamers never experience déjà vu, then its absence may be a warning sign of a sleep disorder that could disrupt memory. There are specific dream periods during every healthy person's sleep called REM (Rapid Eye Movement) which play a crucial role in learning and recall.

On the other hand, too much déjà vu may be a sign of mental illness or an organic brain problem. As we have already seen, some research indicates that déjà vu is more common in bipolar disorder, depression, and schizophrenia. Temporal lobe epileptic seizures, too, have a characteristic déjà vu component.

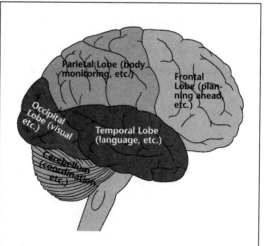

The temporal lobes of the brain are located along the side of the head above the ears. Two of their major functions relate to language, interpreting sounds, and relating sights to past experience but, significantly, only *what* is seen, not *where* it is.

What parts of the brain are responsible?

Recent research on epileptic seizures that originate in the temporal lobe of the brain has yielded insight into a likely anatomical origin of déjà vu. Decades ago, Canadian neuroscientist Wilder Penfield stimulated an area of the temporal lobe in the brain of a fully conscious epileptic patient under local anesthesia by touching that part of the outer cortex with a fine electric probe. The patient reported feeling a "dreamy state" — consisting of vivid memory-like hallucinations and a déjà vu-like sense of having already lived through the present moment. Other experiments since then have shown that déjà vu experiences can be evoked by stimulating the hippocampus and amygdala, which are more primitive brain structures crucially involved in memory and emotion.

The involvement of structures relating to memory and emotion may explain the mix of memory-like sensations and emotional components that déjà vu combines. For some people, déjà vu is perceived as frighteningly eerie, while for others it has an exhilarating quality.

Recent experiments using EEG recordings show that stimulating any of these parts of the brain — the temporal lobe, hippocampus, or amygdala — can trigger a déjà vu experience involving all three regions. Imaging studies also show that this is the same network of brain areas involved in a temporal lobe epileptic seizure.

A tiny epileptic seizure

In a sense, déjà vu is a brief epileptic attack that fails

to spread to enough regions of the brain to trigger a full-blown epileptic seizure. Like the déjà vu experience itself, epileptic seizures are categorized into a "minor" and a "major" type — *petit mal* (literally "little sickness") and *grand mal* ("big sickness") respectively. Petit mal seizures, relatively common in children, consist of a brief experience of "absence" from the immediate surroundings. If the seizure spreads to more parts of the brain, it becomes grand mal. Epileptics with grand mal seizures experience all the terrifying signs of an epileptic fit — the uncontrollable stiffening and jerking of the entire body, followed by immobility and a "mental hangover" that can last well after the seizure itself.

Even little epileptic seizures can involve visual, auditory, or olfactory (smell) hallucinations, as well as automatic chewing and swallowing motions, strange stomach sensations, and a feeling of déjà vu. Dostoevsky, van Gogh, and Rasputin were temporal lobe epileptics. Though no scientific proof exists, some historians have conjectured that other famous figures from history may have suffered from some degree of temporal lobe epilepsy which caused auditory hallucinations or visions. Included among them are Joan of Arc, who claimed that God personally instructed her to save France, and some Old Testament figures such as Abraham who, so the Biblical story goes, heard God tell him to kill his son Isaac. Since the myths of the past are not subject to verification by scientific experiment, attributing the motivation of such historic crusaders to mild epileptic seizures can never be more than an educated guess.

WHERE TO LEARN MORE:

J. Bancaud, F. Brunet-Bourgin, P. Chauvel, and E. Halgren (1994). "Anatomical origin of déjà vu and vivid 'memories' in human temporal lobe epilepsy." Brain 117/1: 71-90.

Sigmund Freud (1900). The Interpretation of Dreams, in Complete Psychological Works, vol. 5, p. 399. London: Hogarth Press.

R. Joseph (1999). "Frontal lobe psychopathology: mania, depression, confabulation, catatonia, perseveration, obsessive compulsions, and schizophrenia." Psychiatry 62: 138-72.

Herman N. Sno et al. (1994). "The inventory of déjà vu experiences assessment." The Journal of Nervous and Mental Disease 182/1: 27-33.

Herman N. Sno and Don H. Linszen (1990). "The déjà vu experience: remembrance of things past?" American Journal of Psychiatry 147/12: 1587-95.

A. Sengoku, M. Toichi, and T. Murai (1997). "Dreamy states and psychoses in temporal lobe epilepsy: mediating role of affect." Psychiatry and Clinical Neurosciences 51/1: 23-6.

DYSLEXIA
An Island of Disability Within an Ocean of Competence

Warning Signs of Dyslexia

Dyslexia is a difficulty learning to read and write among otherwise intelligent, motivated children. It is important to diagnose it early, so that special reading instruction may begin as soon as possible. These are some of the warning signs and symptoms to look for:

Reading and Writing:
- difficulty learning the names of the letters of the alphabet
- difficulty reading single words out of context
- difficulty reading nonsense (made-up) words
- poor spelling
- tendency to reverse the order of letters and sometimes numbers, for example:

    sign-sing   *cart-crate*   *35-53*

- in reading, a tendency to confuse similar-looking words, e.g.:

    was-saw   *bust-dust*   *wet-met*   *on-no*

- difficulty with reading comprehension, but not as much as with reading single words in isolation
- slow reading, either silently or out loud

Language: Spoken and Heard
- in preschool children, a delay in language production or problems with speech articulation
- in school, difficulty with tests or tasks involving rhymes or breaking a word down into parts, e.g.:

    name a word that rhymes with bat

    if you take the b *away from the word* bat, *what are you left with?*

- difficulty breaking down words into syllables or pronounceable parts, e.g.:

    break-fast   *par-ty*   *win-dow*

The Bandleader On Strike

Learning to read and write is an impressively complex process. It draws on a wide variety of skills housed in many different parts of the brain. Some of the circuits for those skills are "hardwired" and some learned, consciously or subconsciously, from experience. The fact that toddlers succeed in learning to speak a native language simply by hearing it spoken around them doesn't mean the process of acquiring all that knowledge is simple. In fact, it can raise our respect for such innate skills when we see something go wrong in the course of acquiring them. Dyslexia is a case in point.

Researchers currently working in this field define dyslexia as an unexpected difficulty in learning to read and write fluently when it occurs in either children or adults who otherwise possess the intelligence, motivation, and schooling considered necessary to master these skills with ease. Parents and teachers of dyslexic children well know that there's more to reading and writing than meets the eye as they watch their intelligent and motivated children struggle to learn the names or sound-values of letters, keep their *d*'s and *b*'s straight, and spell common words.

The cognitive connections involved
Reading involves not just the language areas of the brain's left *temporal* lobe located above the ear, but also the *occipital* lobe, an area towards the back of the brain housing visual centers. Equally important are the regions, structures, and pathways connecting all these areas, the "conductors of the band," so to speak, that enable the language and visual

circuits to communicate freely and rapidly. Some people who have brain damage to one of these connecting regions lose their ability to blend their language and literacy skills together into a seamless whole. They may be able to write, but they are unable to understand what they've written when they read silently. Yet they can read the words they have written out loud with full understanding and they can match letters with their sounds. Because the ability to understand spoken language is intact they can understand written words only when they recite them. The problem arises in reading because the connection between their visual area and the language area that interprets meaning is damaged; but the connection between their visual area and the part of their brain that matches visual symbols to sounds is still functioning.

On a different level of brain circuitry, when a child starts to learn language he learns that words can be formed by linking smaller speech-sounds — the *phonological* component of language. Later, as he learns to write he learns to apply the particular sound-symbol pairings (the sounds that go with letters) conventionally represented in the alphabet used in his language's writing system. A child's reading skill becomes more efficient as he unconsciously begins to recognize more and more written words as visual wholes rather than laboriously building up each word by combining the letter-sounds that form it. When all these associations become highly automated and are performed quickly the learner becomes a fluent reader.

**How is dyslexia different from other learning diffi-
culties children have?**

Along with ADHD (see page 9) and low-level depression, dyslexia is one of those mild brain disorders
that more and more people seem to have these days.
It is the most common of all learning disabilities and
is now estimated, conservatively, as affecting five percent of all children. Some minor brain dysfunctions
can be caused by environmental factors such as early
exposure to pollutants, lead, or malnutrition.
Dyslexia, on the other hand, has a strong genetic
basis. The recent increase in diagnosing reading difficulties as dyslexia is probably due two factors unrelat-
ed to its causes. For one thing, the single term *dyslexia* now replaces a variety of competing terms — *congenital word blindness, developmental alexia, specific
reading disability, Minimal Brain Dysfunction* — used to
refer to dyslexic disabilities since the beginning of the
twentieth century. An increased awareness of the
existence and nature of this disorder among parents
and educators may also account for an increase in
diagnosis in the medical community.

Symptoms of dyslexia (literally "difficult words")
tend to come as a surprise to families because the
general intelligence level and spoken language ability
of the dyslexic individual are typically normal or better. Therefore, dyslexia represents a specific island of
disability within an ocean of competence — roughly
opposite to the condition called *idiot savantism* (see
page 96).

Even though dyslexia has to do with reading and
writing rather than language as a whole, it isn't a

mere visual deficiency. (One reason the earlier term *congenital word blindness* fell out of favor is that there isn't any visual "blindness" for letters — or anything else — in dyslexia.) There is no universal agreement about the exact kind or degree of reading difficulty that needs to be present to justify a diagnosis of dyslexia, but the list on page 60 gives some of the warning signs and symptoms that should prompt a comprehensive evaluation.

Strategies used by older children and adults
People with dyslexia often can develop strategies to compensate for their reading difficulties. For example, even if their ability to break down a relatively unfamiliar word into its component parts is poor, they might be able to identify the word from the context of the passage it appears in. That's why tests for dyslexia require the child to decipher the meaning of a written word which is presented in a list, rather than in a sentence.

Unconsciously, dyslexics often use superior memory skills to disguise reading difficulties — much as a toddler, who cannot yet read, can correct a parent's incorrect reading of a familiar bedtime story. The physician James Hinshelwood, one of the pioneers in dyslexia research, cites the case of an intelligent dyslexic boy who couldn't even read short, common words such as "the" or "of," but relied on his auditory memory to get around his reading difficulties:

> When I first saw the boy and his father at the
> Glasgow Eye Infirmary I asked them to call on me
> at my house and I wrote down the address on an

envelope. A few days thereafter the father could
not find the envelope, but the boy at once repeated the address correctly, having remembered it
from hearing me state it once.

What causes dyslexia?

The *etiology,* or cause, of dyslexia has been a matter of
intense speculation and research for over one hundred years. The complex interaction of brain systems
that cause it has prevented any simple explanation or
treatment. The knack of reading fluently is in itself so
complex, involving so many different sub-circuits in
diverse brain regions, that any problem in any one
area can disrupt the skill as a whole. There is thus
really no one single cause of all instances of dyslexia.

A left-brain problem is the usual explanation

The best-known theory of dyslexia proposes that the
disorder arises from left-hemisphere brain damage in
the womb or abnormal brain hemisphere development. This is plausible because, for most people, the
language centers are concentrated in the left hemisphere of their brain. The theory of left-hemisphere
damage before birth is similar to an influential theory
about one cause of left-handedness (see page 71). If
the left side of the fetus's brain does not develop
properly the normal dominant role of the left hemisphere shifts to the right side of the brain. This shift
of dominant motor control to the right hemisphere
may coincide with changes in left-hemisphere brain
systems that normally control written language processing. The reason the left hemisphere is more vulnerable to underdevelopment before birth is that it
develops later and more slowly, making it more at

risk from factors as widely varied as excess levels of testosterone, competition from a twin, drug abuse by the mother, or breech birth.

Many common abnormalities in brain function besides dyslexia and left-handedness — among them, speech problems, allergies, and ADHD — are also traced to unbalanced development of the two sides of the brain in the womb. There is a striking statistical correlation between all these disorders and left-handedness, in fact. For example, left-handers are more likely to be dyslexic than right-handers. Furthermore, because males are exposed to more testosterone in the womb than females, there is a greater prevalence of left-handedness, ADHD, and dyslexia among males than females, according to current evidence.

The finding that dyslexia may be caused by underdevelopment of the left side of the brain is significant. The left hemisphere excels at linear, analytical, sequential processing of information, while the right is better at "holistic," simultaneous processing. Learning to read relies on both strategies. In the process of learning, children normally come to recognize and process familiar words as one unit, rather than having to break them down into their component letters or letter-groups. That strategy doesn't work with less common or unfamiliar words — such as *meretricious* or the proper name *Katzenellenbogen*. Even adults break those down in more analytical fashion, to translate them into their component letter-sound values. When dyslexics read they tend to be better at whole-word recognition than at breaking words down into their component parts, which is a left-brain task. Poor spelling and letter reversals, common in dyslexia, are another indicator of failure of left-brain data-processing skills.

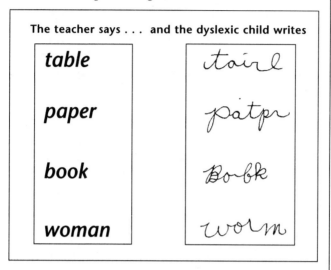

The teacher says . . .	and the dyslexic child writes
table	*taïrl*
paper	*patpr*
book	*Borbk*
woman	*worm*

The box to the left shows the results of a test of a dyslexic boy who has not been able to learn the sounds associated with all the letters of the alphabet. The column on the left are the words dictated to him by the teacher and, to the right, his handwritten response.

What happened to the band leader?

A variety of recent studies shows that dyslexics may be deficient in the processing of both auditory and visual stimuli presented in rapid sequence. In other words, they have a hard time keeping track of the sorts of small bits of information — in whatever sensory domain — that the analytical, linear left hemisphere handles best. Reading a sentence requires that many neurons located in different parts of the brain all fire in unison. A new theory of dyslexia points to poor coordination or communication between those different regions of the brain involved in reading. For example, a recent study out of the London-based Institute of Neurology shows that while performing a reading task, the brains of dyslexics fail to activate all of the left-brain regions that fire in unison in normal brains performing the same task. The apparent reason lies in a weak or missing "band leading" structure located in the left *insula* of the cortex, which performs the essential task of coordinating their firing.

New research suggests that faults in the brain's white matter are interfering with basic circuitry
In the past, brain imaging techniques such as structural MRI permitted detailed analysis of different areas of the "gray matter" of the cerebral cortex, the wrinkled thinking cap of gray matter on the surface of the brain. But those scans could not accurately depict the underlying "white matter," composed of long axons connecting brain cells in widely scattered regions of the cortex. A very recent Stanford University study used a new "diffusion tensor" MRI technology that allows a much more detailed view of the white matter. It revealed that dyslexics may suffer from abnormalities in their white matter tracts that impair the communication not just among different regions within the language-processing area of the left hemisphere, but also among widely-scattered language-processing, visual, and auditory regions of the brain.

The treatment of dyslexia
Dyslexia is not a disease, and there is no "cure" for it. If the "hemisphere" theory of dyslexia has any validity, it may reflect a different way of viewing things — more "holistically," less analytically — rather than a mere deficiency. If, on the other hand, the "communication disconnection" theory offers a valid explanation for at least some types of dyslexia, then it's easier to view the reading and writing difficulties as due to

a disorder. The fact remains that reading and writing are such important skills that failing to learn them fluently can be a significant handicap socially and professionally.

All experts agree that the most important factors in dealing with reading disabilities are early intervention and appropriate treatment. Current evidence supports the conclusion that the longer the problem goes untreated, the harder it is to overcome. For dyslexia, treatment is not so much a matter of making the brain of a dyslexic like that of a non-dyslexic, but of using remedial reading training to help convey the concepts that dyslexics fail to grasp as automatically as non-dyslexics. This means, for example, spending extra time establishing the idea that words can be broken down into smaller sound-units, and that letters of the alphabet match up with these sound-units.

Time for a little help from our friends.
In addition, dyslexia educators as well as dyslexics themselves emphasize that the accommodation between the worlds of dyslexics and non-dyslexics shouldn't be all one-way. Assuming that a dyslexia-type reading disability has nothing to do with a lack of motivation to learn to read fluently, or a lack of self-discipline to understand the ideas that the written passages are intended to convey, it makes sense that the same sorts of adjustments be made for dyslexics as for others with physical handicaps. Thus, dyslexics would not enjoy an unfair advantage if they were allowed extra time to complete a written test, or permitted to demonstrate their knowledge in an oral

exam rather than a written one — especially for dyslexics who are identified so late that they can't benefit from remedial reading programs.

WHERE TO LEARN MORE:

N. Brunswick et al. (1999). "Explicit and implicit processing of words and pseudowords by adult developmental dyslexics." Brain 122: 1901-17.

D.C.M. Gersons-Wolfensberger and Wied A.J.J.M. Ruijssenaars (1997). "Definition and treatment of dyslexia: a report by the committee on dyslexia of the health council of the Netherlands." Journal of Learning Disabilities 30/2: 209-13.

Torkel Klingberg et al. (2000). "Microstructure of temporo-parietal white matter as a basis for reading ability: evidence from diffusion tensor magnetic resonance imaging." Neuron 25: 493-500.

E. Paulesu et al. (1996). "Is developmental dyslexia a disconnection syndrome? Evidence from PET scanning." Brain 119/1: 143-57.

Sally E. Shaywitz (1998). "Dyslexia." The New England Journal of Medicine 338/5: 307-12.

Sally E. Shaywitz et al. (1998). "Functional disruption in the organization of the brain for reading in dyslexia." Proceedings of the National Academy of Sciences (USA) 95: 2636-41.

HANDEDNESS
Left-turn Signals

A Test: What's Your Dominant Foot, Eye, and Ear?

Handedness is only one way in which humans can be asymmetrically "sided." For almost all people, one foot, eye, and ear is dominant as well. Overall, nine of ten people are right-handed; eight of ten are right-footed; seven of ten are right-eyed; and six of ten are right-eared. Women tend to be more right-sided than men in all respects except "eyedness." Determine your dominant foot, eye, and ear by answering these questions:

Foot

(1) Which foot do you kick a ball with?
(2) Try picking up a pen with your toes. Which foot do you use?
(3) If you're starting up a staircase, which foot goes first?

Eye

(1) Select a spot on a wall at least ten feet away. Quickly lift a hand and point to the spot. Then close each eye in turn and see which eye lines up with the finger and the spot. (If you're right-eyed, your finger will be pointing directly at the spot when your left eye is closed.)
(2) Which eye would you use to peep through a keyhole?
(3) Which eye to look down into a dark bottle to see the liquid?

Ear

(1) If you wanted to eavesdrop on a conversation in the next room, which ear would you press against the wall?
(2) In a noisy, crowded place, which side of your head would you turn toward a companion to hear her better?
(3) If you want to hear the "ocean" sound in a seashell, which ear would you hold the shell to?

If your results are mixed, that's typical. Fewer people are strongly right-footed, right-eyed, and right-eared than strongly right-handed; less than half of all people are consistently one-sided (either left or right) in everything.

Left-Sidedness: Its Causes and Consequences

Left-handers have always had a lot to put up with. They've been on the losing end of right-handed appliances, backhanded compliments, insulting metaphors, cross-culturally widespread prejudices, not to mention countless old and tired jokes. The view from the hard, cold world of mathematical probability doesn't get any better. Statistically they're also more likely to die younger, have learning disorders such as dyslexia and ADHD (see pages 59 and 9 respectively). Further, they are more likely to have immune system or autoimmune problems such as asthma or diabetes, to be anxious and antisocial, and even be alcoholics. Left-handed women are also more likely to undergo menopause at a younger age than right-handers.

On the other hand, left-handers are overrepresented among chess experts, architects, artists, and applied mathematicians.

Are you a "pathological" left-hander?

An explanation for all of these puzzling patterns comes from the theory that there are two kinds of left-handedness, genetic and "pathological." Left-handedness does appear to have some genetic basis; if one or more of your parents is left-handed, chances are increased that you'll be a lefty as well. More precisely, if neither of your parents is left-handed, your chances of being a left-hander are about one in ten. If just your mother is left-handed, chances are double — two in ten — that you'll be left-handed. If both parents are lefties, chances are three to four in ten that you will be, too.

A Thumbnail Sketch Sherlock Holmes could have employed this odd, but not wholly reliable, way to tell if murder victims were right-or left-handed. Examine their thumbnails. The larger and more square-shaped of the two nails reveals the dominant hand, according to published research. Other research based on this hypothesis is conflicting.

But some left-handedness appears to be pathological — the result of brain damage in the womb. Since connections between the brain and body are largely crossed or *contralateral*, left-handedness indicates dominant motor or muscle control by the right side of the brain. If a problem occurs during the development of the brain's left hemisphere, dominant motor control may shift to the right, resulting in left-handedness. If some left-handedness is indeed caused by brain damage, then it's not surprising that it correlates with other brain-based problems.

Conversely, if a problem occurred during the development of the right hemisphere, then it stands to reason that someone genetically predisposed to be a lefty would end up being a "pathological" right-hander. But if you do the math, you'll see why there would be far fewer pathological right-handers than pathological left-handers. Assuming that about ten percent of people are genetically predisposed to be lefties, and, say, ten percent of those "natural" left-handers have some sort of brain damage that would lead to their handedness being switched, only one percent of people overall would be pathological right-handers. But if 90 percent of people are natural right-handers, and ten percent of those have left-hemisphere brain damage, then nine percent of the population would end up being pathological left-handers.

There's another reason why more left-handedness

than right-handedness might be pathological. The brain's left hemisphere develops later, and more slowly, than the right. So there's more opportunity for a problem in the womb to harm the left hemisphere. The left hemisphere is also more vulnerable to damage in the womb, just as it is later in life, because of asymmetries in blood supply. (That's one reason left-hemisphere strokes have more serious consequences for older adults than right-hemisphere strokes.)

Testosterone: bad for the brain

One likely culprit in the brain-damage scenario is testosterone, a hormone that can be harmful to the developing brain. Testosterone can also injure the thymus, a gland that regulates the body's immune and autoimmune systems. Since male fetuses are exposed to higher levels of testosterone than females, this may explain why men are one and a half times as likely to be left-handed than women.

Another theory holds that left-handedness is often a result of birth stress, including trauma in the womb and difficult birth. Premature birth, prolonged labor, breech birth, and low birth weight are all risk factors for developmental problems and increase the chance of left-handedness. Twins are more likely to be left-handed as well, probably because competition for nutrients and stressful delivery increase the chances of difficulties for left-brain development. Those same influences correlate with higher than normal incidence of autism, epilepsy, cerebral palsy, Down Syndrome, and even schizophrenia.

Who is a Lefty?
When the survey results from an early but important study of over a million subjects were compiled they revealed the following statistics:
• Men are more likely (12.6%) to be left-handed than women (9.9%).
• Young people (i.e. 10-20 years old) are more likely to be left-handed (14% for men, 12% for women) than are the elderly (near 6% for both sexes).
• 11% of Americans and Europeans are left-handed.
• People of Asian (9.3%) or Hispanic (9.1%) lineage are slightly less likely to be left-handed than whites, blacks, or Native Americans.

Does having a brain that's "backwards" for motor control imply other brain differences?

One of the best-known generalizations about brain asymmetry is that the main language centers — controlling both the understanding and the production of speech — are in the left half of the brain. Most lefties, like most right-handers, have left-brain language centers. However, the asymmetry isn't as pronounced as it is for right-handers: while 97 percent of right-handers have left-brain speech centers, 68 percent of left-handers do. An additional 12 percent of lefties have speech centers that are bilateral, or fairly evenly distributed across both hemispheres. That leaves 20 percent of left-handers with right-brain language control, as opposed to just three percent of right-handers.

Do left-handers think differently or tend to have different skills?

Handedness researchers Coren and Clare Porac have shown that left-handed university students are more likely to major in visually-based, as opposed to language-based, subjects. Another sample of 103 art students, an astounding 47 percent were left- or mixed-handed. Since art, architecture and chess rely heavily on right-brain-based visual skills, it may be that a right hemisphere that dominates for motor skills may tend to correlate with unusually strong abilities in other right-brain-based skills.

Actuarial and other data bearing on life-affecting correlations with left-sidedness

At age 15, right-handers outnumber left-handers 7 to 1, but by the age of 85 the right-to-left-handed ratio has changed to 200-1! One explanation is that somehow left-handers became right-handers as they grew older, though no evidence supports this. Research by psychologist Stanley Coren indicates that older left-handers are not found in these studies simply because they are not there to find. New research shows a higher than average accident rate among left-handers whose deaths from accidental injury results in 36 life-years lost; cancer 16, heart failure and stroke combined, only 12.

A recent discovery from research using laboratory mice suggests a cause of left-sided dominance
It is true that the children of parents who are left-handed are often also left handed, yet about 20 percent of identical twins differ in handedness even though they are as genetically identical as clones. How can that be? Some recent work by Amar Klar at the National Cancer Institute has shown that a mutant strain of mice lacks a specific gene that is present in all other mice. When those mutant mice mate, half of their offspring have their hearts on the left, as normal mice do, but half of them are born with their hearts on their right sides. In humans, this finding suggests that the identical twins with different handedness also lack a gene that normally causes right-sided dominance so they have an even chance of going either way. Dr. Klar is currently researching that very point. Still, his theory of a "right-handed" gene is inconsistent with statistics showing that left handed mothers are more likely to have left- than right-handed sons and that more men than women are left-handed. There are so many factors that can impact a structure as incredibly complex as the human brain that such, well, incredible, theories often turn out to be true as increasingly sophisticated technologies equip continuing research.

Several studies have shown that left-handers are not only more apt to be smokers than right-handers, but also more likely to become alcoholics, with a poorer prognosis for recovering from alcoholism. EEG imaging technology also reveals that left-handers tend to have a stronger brain response to a wide variety of prescription and over-the-counter medications as well, which may explain their cognitive susceptibility to alcohol and nicotine addiction.

WHERE TO LEARN MORE:

M. Annett and M.P. Alexander (1996). "Atypical cerebral dominance: predictions and tests of the right shift theory." Neuropsychologia 34: 1215-27.

J.E. Block (1974). "Thumbs down on left-handedness." New England Journal of Medicine 291/6: 307.

M.P. Bryden, I.C. McManus, and B. Bulman-Fleming (1994). "Evaluating the empirical support for the Geschwind-Behan-Galaburda model of cerebral lateralization." Brain and Cognition 26: 103-67.

M.C. Corballis (1980). "Laterality and myth." American Psychologist 35: 284-295.

S. Coren (1993). The Left-Hander Syndrome. New York: Vintage.

S. Coren (1995). "Family patterns in handedness: evidence for indirect inheritance mediated by birth stress." Behavioral Genetics 25/6: 517-24.

S. Dane, N. Reis, and T. Pasinliogut (1999). "Left-handed women have earlier age of menopause." Journal of Basic Clinical Physiological Pharmacology 10/2: 147-50.

J.T. DeKay (1994). The Left-Hander's Handbook. New York: Book-of-the-Month Club Inc.

A.N. Gilbert and C.J. Wysocki (1992). "Hand preference and age in the United States." Neuropsychologia 30/7: 601-8.

P. Irwin (1985). "Greater brain response of left-handers to drugs." Neuropsychologia 23/1: 61-7.

PERFECT PITCH
Tuned In the Genes

When a Brain Tunes In

The unusual brain that is naturally tuned to musical tones — this gift of perfect pitch — is evidence, yet again, that the physical structure of the brain accounts for differences in people's capacities to perform specific tasks. Such differences may sometimes be present at birth. Even if they are not, when a person persistently demands that his or her brain perform a specific task, that person's brain may also change to become more similar to the naturally gifted one. The key point is this: when we make demands on our brain it changes *physically* to meet those demands. That change, in turn, increases our brain's capacity to perform.

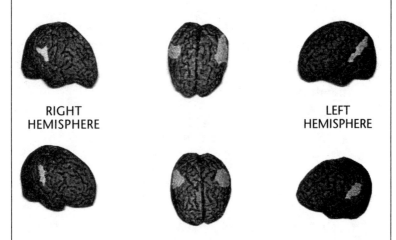

RIGHT
HEMISPHERE

LEFT
HEMISPHERE

The MRI brain scans, above, show structural differences in the planum temporale of musicians with perfect pitch (upper row) and non-musicians (lower row). In musicians with perfect pitch, the planum temporale (light area) is considerably larger in the left hemisphere than the right. In non-musicians, and in musicians without perfect pitch, the left planum temporale is only slightly larger than the right (see page 85).

Nurture as Nature's Partner

There's a story about Wolfgang Amadeus Mozart visiting a farm as a two-year-old. Upon hearing a pig squeal, the future composer cried out "G sharp!" When someone ran inside to check the child's exuberant identification on the piano, it turned out little Mozart was absolutely right.

Mozart had what is known as *perfect* (or *absolute*) *pitch* — the ability to identify the pitch of a tone without the use of another known note as a reference point. Perfect pitch is rare, even among professional musicians. Its frequency of occurrence is estimated to be less than one in 10,000. Musical training doesn't lead to perfect pitch ability. Rather, perfect pitch seems to be something along the lines of a gift, much like photographic or eidetic memory (see page 88). That's why so few musicians have it, even those with outstanding creativity and skill.

It is difficult to test for the gift of perfect pitch
If perfect pitch is really an inborn trait independent of musical training, then you might expect non-musicians to have it as frequently as musicians. This hypothesis turns out to be difficult to test as a practical matter. First, any test of non-musicians' perfect pitch ability would have to involve extremely large numbers of subjects because the gift is so rare. Second, the usual way to identify the pitch of a tone is with a label (*B flat,* etc.) that must be learned as part of the study of music. Therefore every one of the subjects in a test would have to have learned those formal labels for all notes, or how could the experimenter check their pitch skills?

Musical training cannot create perfect pitch, but it does build on an inborn ability

Investigators have designed an objective mechanical task that neutralizes the fact that some of the subjects they need to test have never learned the nomenclature for musical scales. They ask such a subject to identify the pitch of a tone by adjusting the knob on an oscillator until it matches the pitch of a tone he's heard. If he can match the tone precisely in this way, his identification of it is perfect, and he might be considered to have perfect pitch.

Even this procedure has a hitch. Not all people who can *identify* a tone absolutely can also *reproduce* it absolutely. Also, some experiments still inadvertently favor those who can attach a label to a tone. For example, scientists can measure how long it takes before someone forgets a specific tone they've heard a day or more before. Such tests show that people with perfect pitch have much better memory than those without perfect pitch. The reason, though, for that superior pitch memory turns out to be that only those with perfect pitch can readily attach a *label* — the name of the note — to the tone they've heard. It's the concrete verbal name-tag, then — *F sharp*, etc. — that serves to reinforce their memory for the exact tone they heard.

Another difficulty such an experiment might encounter is that, even if the only people found to have perfect pitch were musicians, that still wouldn't mean that perfect pitch is learned through musical training as opposed to being innate. Many innate skills show themselves only if the individual born with them receives training in some form at a young age. Perfect pitch may well be such a skill. Perhaps this is why the only reports claiming that perfect pitch was taught relates to very young children, between three and six years of age.

Why even babies can be Beatles fans

If, as it appears to be, perfect pitch really is an innate ability that shows up in many different cultures, then it ties in with other inborn aspects of musical skill. The ability to perform music and recognize specific musical forms is an acquired skill based on the kind of music the musician grows up listening to, but it also taps into deep-seated innate knowledge. Here is a convincing proof of that idea. The intervals familiar to fans of the Beatles or Beethoven make sense to babies who haven't yet had the chance to learn these specific expressions of the universal musical language. When experimenters play series of musical intervals to six-month-old infants, the infants key in on changes between perfect 4ths or 5ths. The concept of the octave — that is, that two notes of different frequency can still count as the same — has also proven to be universal. It is based on an innate ability to perceive that one note and a second note with a completely different sound are the same — except that the second has exactly double the sound-wave frequency of the first.

The "musical" elements of languages — the tones of Cantonese and Swahili, for example — are easy for infants to master. An adult English speaker must use analytical left-brain skills to master such strange

Starting Young
Now, some researchers even claim that the potential for perfect pitch is something we're *all* born with. Whether we actually develop it or not has to do with whether we receive appropriate musical training from a young age. With this in mind, it's interesting to note that most musicians with perfect pitch started their musical training before age seven.

Baby Babble
All babies, the world over, are born with a delicate sensitivity to variations in pitch. This may account for the remarkable fact that when a mother or other caretaker in *any* culture speaks to her baby she uses the same dramatic changes in the pitch of her voice — never a flat monotone.

tone systems — a frustrating and intimidating task. To an infant it comes naturally to use a listen-and-learn experimental approach. What is more, as their brains continue to develop into their language-leaning years, the quantity of brain cells they have to apply to the job are growing at a furious pace.

Home plate for the perfect pitch

A recent brain-scan study by a leading music-and-brain researcher has even identified the precise locus in the brain of perfect pitch ability. With the use of MRI, a technology that permits detailed analysis of brain structure, Gottfried Schlaug and colleagues found that a brain region called the *planum temporale* (the sides, just above the ears, of the brain's outer cortex) is larger not only in musicians with perfect pitch than in non-musicians — but also larger than in trained musicians who *don't* have perfect pitch (see page 80.)

In almost all people, the planum temporale in the left side of the brain specializes in processing language. For that reason it is normally larger than its counterpart in the right side. Music, in contrast to language, is proving to be largely a right-brain ability. People with left-hemisphere strokes that render them unable to speak may still be able to sing a song, words and all, but right-brain damage can prevent that person from recognizing a familiar melody. Right-brain stroke patients may also lose their ability to handle "melodic" aspects of language — such as intonation — resulting in monotonous, seemingly emotionless speech.

Are musicians born with a larger left temporal area or does their music enlarge it?

Some recent studies using PET (positron emission tomography) scans have shown that innate musical ability — the kind of born-with-it skill that allows us to recognize and remember the "Polly Wolly Doodle" tune — depends mostly on the right hemisphere. Certain more sophisticated skills, on the other hand — composing music, analyzing the details of a composition — are more left-brain-based.

In the Schlaug study of perfect pitch, the left temporal lobe of the brain was significantly larger in musicians than in non-musicians. However, if you subtract the perfect pitch possessors from the general group of musicians, that difference in size all but disappears. In other words, almost all of the size difference is due to the musicians with perfect pitch.

A different kind of evidence pointing to the status of perfect pitch as an innate ability largely independent of musical training comes from studies of musical *savants* (people with a remarkable degree of natural specialized ability). Over half of all autistic savants are gifted in music. (For more information on autistic

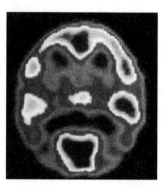

Scans of human brains show increased activity when listening to music (right), especially in the temporal area to the side, compared to a brain when resting with no stimulus. PET scans like these measure the rate at which the brain burns glucose "fuel." A white area shows activity. The dark area within the white reveals the highest level of glucose consumption.

skills see page 44.) Though most do not have perfect pitch, reports of perfect pitch are much more common among this group than among the general population. In savants, then — some with low overall IQ scores — perfect pitch seems sometimes to go along with other kinds of impressive musical ability that emerge spontaneously, without formal training.

WHERE TO LEARN MORE:

Stefan Evers et al. (1999). "The cerebral haemodynamics of music perception." Brain 122: 75-85.

Y. Hirata, S. Kuriki, and C. Pantev (1999). "Musicians with absolute pitch show distinct neural activities in the auditory cortex." Neuroreport 10/5: 599-1002.

Rachel Nowak (1995). "Brain center linked to perfect pitch." Science 267: 616.

Gottfried Schlaug et al. (1995). "In vivo evidence of structural brain asymmetry in musicians." Science 267: 699-701.

J. Sloboda, B. Hermelin, and N. O'Connor (1985). "An exceptional musical memory." Musical Perception 3: 155-70.

Annie H. Takeuchi and Stewart H. Hulse (1993). "Absolute pitch." Psychological Bulletin 113: 345-61.

M. Tervaniemi et al. (1999)."Functional specialization of the human auditory cortex in processing phonetic and musical sounds: a magnetoencephalographic (MEG) study." Neuroimage 9: 330-6.

R.L. Young and T. Nettlebeck (1995). "The abilities of a musical savant and his family." Journal of Autism and Developmental Disorders 25/3: 231-47.

PHOTOGRAPHIC MEMORY
Data, Data Everywhere

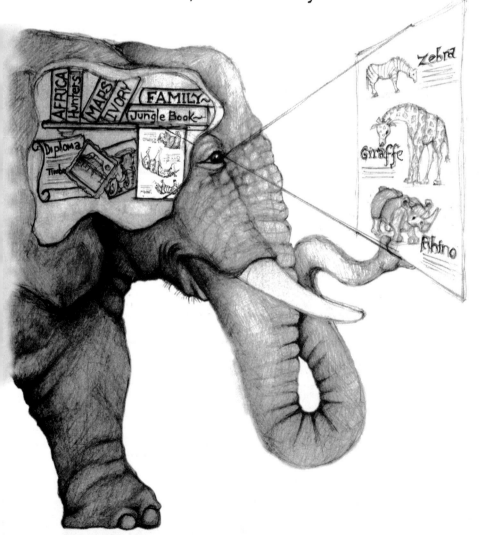

A Test: Eidetic Memory

There are many degrees of the memory capacity generally called "photographic," some so unique that they have names of their own. An *eidetic* memory (see page 97) is one of those. This is a test that reveals that capacity.

First, study the assortment of dots in the top box for about thirty seconds. Let your eyes scan all parts of the picture, rather than fixating on just one spot. Then, do the same with the assortment of dots in the second box. Does a word reveal itself? See page 90 for the answer.

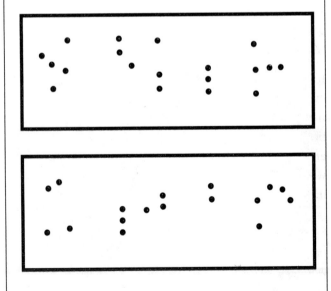

A Camera in the Brain

In his fictional essay "Funes, the Memorious," Argentine writer Jorge Luis Borges describes a man who has such a prodigious memory for details that "it was not only difficult for him to understand that the generic term *dog* embraced so many unlike specimens of different forms; he was disturbed by the fact that a dog at 3:14 PM (seen in profile) should have the same name as the dog at 3:15 PM (seen from the front)."

The paradox of photographic memory

Would you really *want* to remember everything? This, in a nutshell, is the downside of a skill so uncommonly strong that it interferes with itself. For most of us, detailed information is committed to memory only after effortful study. The human brain is ingeniously designed to block most incoming data from being noticed and moved into memory storage. When storage happens without conscious effort it is generally because of a strong, perhaps survival-related, emotional component.

Imagine what it would be like to receive an e-mail every ten seconds and never being able to take a break from having to read and file it immediately — whether or not it was important. No matter how sharp you are and how good your computer, you'd soon be over-whelmed by clutter.

A person with eidetic memory could have seen this word by superimposing the two boxes of dots shown on page 88.

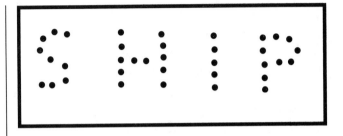

One of the most intriguing descriptions of someone with a photographic memory comes from the Russian neurologist A.R. Luria's account of the mnemonic genius S.V. Shereshevskii (see box on page 91). Shereshevskii had such a remarkable visual memory that he could not only memorize a table of fifty numbers in less than three minutes, but also retain that grid in his memory for the rest of his life — along with thousands of other grids he had memorized as a professional mnemonic performer.

Memorization techniques used by "natural" photographic memorizers are relatively effortless and automatic. In Shereshevskii's case, all he would do would be to stare at the table, close his eyes to check if the visual image was fixed in his mind, and then stare again if the image was poorly fixed or incomplete. Once the process was over, he could just as easily read out the numbers, from memory, in reverse order as from top to bottom, or just as easily read out diagonal rows as horizontal rows. And if he was tested, completely without warning, thirty years later, Shereshevskii would recall the number-table just as flawlessly as on the day he had first committed it to memory.

A CASE HISTORY

The Most Astounding Memory of Them All

One of the most intriguing descriptions of a *mnemonic* (memory-related) genius comes from the Russian neurologist A.R. Luria's account of his astounding countryman S.V. Shereshevskii. Shereshevskii was a professional mnemonic performer with a memory, in Luria's words, that was "one of the keenest the literature on the subject has ever described."

Since Shereshevskii's amazing gift was in *visual* memory, he would have to use a special translation technique — for example, the classical Greek orator's trick described on page 92 — if he wanted to memorize sounds. This method was so literally visual for Shereshevskii that the only trouble he had was if he placed one of the objects in a location where he might overlook it — say, placing a white object against a white background or a dark object too far from a street lamp in a poorly lit alley. That's why Luria attributed any errors Shereshevskii made in his recollections not to mistakes of *memory,* but mistakes of *perception.*

In addition to his powers of visual memory, he had a rich *synesthetic* ability (see page 111), which served as an automatic signal to him if he ever recalled a word inaccurately. Since each word would have a distinct taste, texture, or sound associated with it, he would recognize right away if he had substituted a synonym for the actual word first read to him. That is, if a word he thought was on the list did not call up the correct parallel sensory association, he would know it was incorrect.

6 6 8 0
5 4 3 2
1 6 8 4
7 9 3 5
4 2 3 7
3 8 9 1
1 0 0 2
3 4 5 1
2 7 6 8
1 9 2 6
2 9 6 7
5 5 2 0
0 1

How long
would it take
you to
memorize
the entire
table
above?...

A trick for enhancing memory

For someone with a specifically *visual* photographic memory, a somewhat more elaborate procedure is required for memorizing sounds. One technique is to translate the sounds into a visual mode, which can then be memorized automatically. This Classical Greek orator's trick works for many people (including those of us with only average visual memory skills): place the object each word represents along a visual mental path (say, familiar city streets, or various rooms in your house). Once you do that, all you have to do is mentally stroll down that path and observe each object as you go, calling out its name as you pass it.

The flip side of a detailed photographic memory

For photographic memorizers, all the details that their steel-trap memory retains can also *interfere* with attention and recall. For one thing, when memorizing a grid of numbers, they might fail to notice any pattern in the grid that most people would automatically notice and use to memorize the table as a whole. For example, they might use their usual camera-like technique to memorize a table with a first line "1, 2, 3, 4," a second line "2, 3, 4, 5," and so on.

And for a photographic memorizer who also has *synesthetic* powers (see page 116), the images that particular words evoke in an ordinary conversation have little or nothing to do with the point of an utterance. He might therefore often feel overwhelmed and confused in the course of a conversation, or when reading a book.

Another type of problem that the memory-artist Shereshevskii encountered during his performances was also due to his synesthetic abilities. If somebody in the audience sneezed or coughed while he was attempting to fix a number-table visually in his memory, a smear or smudge would suddenly appear and obscure some part of the table in his mind's eye.

A photographic memory — but trouble remembering faces

In addition — much like Borges' character Funes — photographic memorizers often so lack the ability to abstract away from specific details that they have a poor memory for faces. As Shereshevskii put it:

> They're so changeable. A person's expression depends on his mood and on the circumstances under which you happen to meet him. People's faces are constantly changing; it's the different shades of expression that confuse me and make it so hard to remember faces.

What some professional performers of feats of recall try to do, then, is to dampen their gift offstage so it does not become a curse of everyday life. They can be plagued for years by their inability to forget meaningless number-tables and random word and number sequences they had once memorized. They lack the typical human ability to extract patterns from the details of life, and to remember just those patterns as the details themselves are forgotten. So while one aspect of their memory is extraordinary, another can be deficient. (The same often applies to *autistic savants;* see pages 45-47.)

...Shereshevskii needed just three minutes of study to recall and, with no errors, name all the numbers in the table on the opposite page.

A CASE HISTORY

Tape-recorder Memory

Not all photographic memory is strictly "photographic" in the sense of being visual. Austrian-born simultaneous interpreter Hans Eberstark had an auditorily-based genius for both languages and numbers. Once he registered in memory the sound and meaning of any word in any language — that *qamots'* means "ocean" in Kashaya Pomo, say — he would never forget it.

Eberstark was also a phenomenal mental calculator and number memorizer. His personal technique — more or less the reverse of Shereshevskii's — was to translate numbers into "words" in a language of his own invention. The number 7, for example, would correspond to the sound of the letter L, since it looks like an L upside-down. A sequence of numbers then becomes a sequence of sounds. With this straightforward and entirely automatic translation from number symbols into sound, combined with his photographic auditory memory, Eberstark was able to memorize the first 10,000 digits of *pi*. You remember, 3.14159265358979323846264338327950288419716939937510582097...

Since those few individuals who are gifted with photographic memory have the opposite problem from most of us — they find it hard to forget, rather than to remember — it makes sense that the explanation for their ability may lie in a reversal of normal memory processes. A prevailing theory is that at least some kinds of photographic memory stem from a failure in the swift metabolism of short-term memory. What does this mean? Or, to put it another way....

What you don't need to know, you usually forget
Most everyday, run-of-the-mill life experiences — the phone number you just dialed, or the name of the song that just played on the radio — are easy to remember for a few seconds or minutes. That's called a short-term memory. Only a small fraction of short-term memories become permanently stored in our brain as long-term memories. Recent brain research has shown that a molecule called CREB switches on the production of proteins to form pathways linking brain cells. On a structural level, that's how long-term memories are created.

The reason not every experience gets coded as a permanent memory is that CREB has a twin — call it "anti-CREB" — that normally switches off the protein-synthesis process; that way, your brain isn't overwhelmed with memories of every trivial experience you ever have. Fortunately the CREB molecule has a longer life than anti-CREB. When a stimulus is repeated over and over the CREB levels are able to rise above those of anti-CREB, so that long-term memories are formed. That's why practice and repetition are a good way to learn something new.

To say that the metabolism of short-term memory is swift means that it gets out of our system quickly. If some fact or experience isn't deemed important enough, we forget it, just as a stamp collector might reject a stamp that isn't unusual or valuable enough. What may be happening in the brain of someone with photographic memory is that the structures that automatically metabolize, or get rid of, those trivial bits of data aren't working right, perhaps due to a CREB system imbalance.

Why do some idiot savants have a prodigious memory?

Given the overlap between the phenomenon of photographic memory and that of *idiot savantism* — a combination of low intelligence with some specific, typically memory-related extraordinary ability — it stands to reason that they might sometimes have a common cause. Since there is evidence for abnormalities among some savants in memory-related brain structures — the hippocampus and amygdala, in particular — an explanation of photographic memory in terms of a failure of short-term memory metabolism makes sense.

Another explanation for some autistic savants, confirmed by brain-scan studies, proposes left-hemisphere damage with a compensation by right-brain skills. Since it's the left hemisphere that is primarily involved in abstraction and symbolization, while the right is more "literal-minded," this additional explanation — which isn't in conflict with the first — also makes sense in connection with mnemonic geniuses like Shereshevskii.

A common type of photographic memory your child may well have

A somewhat more modest, and much more common, version of Shereshevskii's kind of visual memory is what is called *eidetic* imagery. (Eidetic comes from the Greek for "pertaining to images.") Eidetikers (those who have this ability) comprise about five percent of children under the age of ten. Since many children lose their eidetic ability as they age, the percentages are lower among the general adult population, but still much higher than for photographic memory.

Eidetic imagery is the persistence of a detailed visual image of a picture for about a minute after it has been examined. It is different from run-of-the-mill visual memory. Eidetikers literally see the image after the picture has been removed. In order to see

A Test: Do You Have Adult Eidetic Powers?

Study the Necker cube below for about thirty seconds. Let your eyes scan all parts of the cube. Then, move your eyes to the blank box below the cube. Only eidetikers can mentally switch the orientation of the image back and forth against the blank canvas of the lower box, so that the gray face is seen as at the front one moment, and at the back the next.

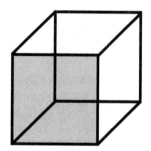

A TEST: **Is Your Child an Eidetiker?**

Eidetic imagery is much more common among young children than among adults. Show your child this picture, and ask her to study it for about thirty seconds. Tell her to look at all parts of the picture, not just one spot.

Then, cover the picture, tell her to look at the blank box to the right, and ask her if she can still see the picture. If she says she can, ask her to describe the picture, followed by more specific questions such as "How many girls are there?" and "How many plates of cookies are there?"

the eidetic image, eidetikers have to look at a blank version of the picture's original background — rather than, for example, being able to see the image when they simply look away or close their eyes. They can mentally move the image sideways on this background, but if they move it to the edge the eidetic image "falls off" and disappears.

Seeing stars: afterimages

Eidetic images also differ from the common visual effect known as an *afterimage*. To see an afterimage, all you have to do is stare at a single point of an image (say, a black star against a white background) for about thirty seconds. The original image is temporarily "burned" onto your eye's retina, so that if you then look at a blank sheet of paper or close your eyes you'll still see the image, but as a negative. (In other words, if you first look at a dark star on a white background, you'll get an afterimage of a white star on a dark background.) If the original image is colored, the afterimage will feature complementary colors (green rather than red, for example).

True eidetic images are always positive, not negative or complementary. Also, while afterimages depend on your fixating on a single point in a picture, eidetic images do not. Eidetikers can scan all parts

To see an afterimage, stare at the center of this black diamond for thirty seconds, then move your eyes to the blank space below.

of a detailed picture and get an eidetic image that they can then scan, moving their eyes from one part of the eidetic image to another, just as they did with the original.

Even though eidetic ability is sometimes referred to as a kind of photographic memory, it definitely does not translate into phenomenal or even above-average memory skills. For one thing, eidetic images fade after a minute or so. For another, some of the tricks or methods that usually help in long-term memory formation actually interfere with eidetic imagery.

If an eidetiker names, labels, or verbally rehearses the items in a picture, for example, he won't get an eidetic image at all. Conversely, if an eidetiker successfully creates an eidetic image, that means he won't have created any sort of verbal encoding that might otherwise help in remembering the original picture.

Words usually help you remember images, and vice-versa

How might verbal encoding help in memorizing an image? Let's take a simple example of a picture composed of a banana, an apple, and a mango in a fruit basket. If you were to take the first letter of the name of each fruit, you could create a word such as "bam." You could then combine this with a new visual image — say, a fruit basket exploding — to help you later work backwards to the individual fruits themselves, so that you could remember exactly what was in the original picture. Since this kind of mnemonic trick would be available to an eidetiker only if he suppressed his eidetic ability, his memory of an image may well be worse than that of a non-eidetiker, once the eidetic image has faded after a minute or so.

A "primitive" ability?

Eidetic imagery is particularly common among brain-damaged children, including hydrocephalics (born with "water on the brain"). This bolsters a theory that eidetic imagery, like photographic memory, might be a sort of developmentally "primitive" ability. That may also be why eidetic imagery is so much more common among children than adolescents and adults.

WHERE TO LEARN MORE:

Erol F. Giray, Warren M. Altkin, and Allan G. Barclay (1976). "Frequency of eidetic imagery among hydrocephalic children." Perceptual and Motor Skills 43: 187-94.

Erol F. Giray, Warren M. Altkin, Glen M Vaught, and Paul A. Roodin (1976). "The incidence of eidetic imagery as a function of age." Child Development 47: 1207-10.

Joseph Glicksohn, Orna Salinger, and Anat Roychman (1992). "An exploratory study of syncretic experience: Eidetics, synaesthesia and absorption." Perception 21: 637-42.

F. Guérin, B. Ska, and S. Belleville (1999). "Cognitive processing of drawing abilities." Brain and Cognition 1999 Aug 40/3: 464-78.

A.R. Luria (1968). The Mind of a Mnemonist. New York: Basic Books.

Steve Miller and Ray Peacock (1982). "Evidence for the uniqueness of eidetic imagery." Perceptual and Motor Skills 55: 1219-33.

SEASONAL AFFECTIVE DISORDER

Or Only the Winter Blues

Seasonal Pattern Assessment Questionnaire (SPAQ)

The SPAQ was developed in the mid-1990's at the National Institute of Mental Health to measure individual's reactions to the seasons. See page 109 for guidance in interpreting responses.

The purpose of this form is to find out how your mood and behavior change over time. Please fill in all the relevant circles. Note: We are interested in your experience; not others you may have observed.

1. In the following questions, fill in circles for all applicable months. This may be a single month ●, a cluster of months, E.G., ●●●, or any other grouping.
   At what time of year do you . . .

	J a n	F e b	M a r	A p r	M a y	J u n	J u l	A u g	S e p	O c t	N o v	D e c		
A Feel best	○	○	○	○	○	○	○	○	○	○	○	○	○	
B Tend to gain most weight	○	○	○	○	○	○	○	○	○	○	○	○	○	
C Socialize most	○	○	○	○	○	○	○	○	○	○	○	○	○	
D Sleep least	○	○	○	○	○	○	○	○	○	○	○	○	○	
E Eat most	○	○	○	○	○	○	○	○	○	○	○	○	○	
F Lose most weight	○	○	○	○	○	○	○	○	○	○	○	○	○	
G Socialize least	○	○	○	○	○	○	○	○	○	○	○	○	○	
H Feel worst	○	○	○	○	○	○	○	○	○	○	○	○	○	
I Eat least	○	○	○	○	○	○	○	○	○	○	○	○	○	
J Sleep most	○	○	○	○	○	○	○	○	○	○	○	○	○	

OR

No particular month(s) stand out as extreme on a regular basis

2. To what degree do the following change with the seasons?
   (ONE CIRCLE ONLY FOR EACH QUESTION)

	0 NO CHANGE	1 SLIGHT CHANGE	2 MODERATE CHANGE	3 MARKED CHANGE	4 EXTREMELY MARKED CHANGE
A Sleep length	○	○	○	○	○
B Social activity	○	○	○	○	○
C Mood (overall feeling of well being)	○	○	○	○	○
D Weight	○	○	○	○	○
E Appetite	○	○	○	○	○
F Energy level	○	○	○	○	○

3. If you experience changes with the seasons, do you feel that these are a problem for you? . . . . ○ No ○ Yes

	MILD	MODERATE	MARKED	SEVERE	DISABLING
If yes, is this problem	○	○	○	○	○

4. By how much does your weight fluctuate during the course of the year?
   ○ 0–3 lbs.
   ○ 4–7 lbs.
   ○ 8–11 lbs.
   ○ 12–15 lbs.
   ○ 16–20 lbs.
   ○ Over 20 lbs.

5. Approximately how many hours of each 24-hour day do you sleep during each season? (Include naps)

Hours slept per day — OVER 18 HOURS

○ WINTER (Dec 21–Mar 20) ⓪①②③④⑤⑥⑦⑧⑨⑩⑪⑫⑬⑭⑮⑯⑰ ○

○ SPRING (Mar 21–June 20) ⓪①②③④⑤⑥⑦⑧⑨⑩⑪⑫⑬⑭⑮⑯⑰ ○

○ SUMMER (June 21–Sept 20) ⓪①②③④⑤⑥⑦⑧⑨⑩⑪⑫⑬⑭⑮⑯⑰ ○

○ FALL (Sept 21–Dec 20) ⓪①②③④⑤⑥⑦⑧⑨⑩⑪⑫⑬⑭⑮⑯⑰ ○

6. Do you notice a change in food preference during the different seasons? . . . . ○ No ○ Yes

Please specify:
_____
_____
_____

IT'S NOT JUST YOUR IMAGINATION

Everyone who spends part of the year in a cold climate knows that it's not unusual for people to feel a little more "down" in the winter than in the summer — an experience some have described as a kind of "emotional hibernation." But for others winter can bring on a much more acute form of the common winter blues, a condition that triggers severe depression and sometimes even suicide. It has recently acquired a name: Seasonal Affective Disorder, or SAD.

Since there are differences in opinion about how severe the symptoms need to be to qualify as SAD, figures for the prevalence of the disorder vary. A middle-of-the-road estimate would place the rate of severe winter depression sufferers in America at about four to six percent, with mild SAD ranging from 10 to 20 percent of the population. The further north or south of the equator one travels, the higher the prevalence of SAD. It is much more common in Minnesota and Alaska than it is in Florida and Arizona. This is not due to cold temperatures, but to a reduction in the amount of sunlight reaching the brain through the eyes.

As the hours of daylight in high-latitude climates drop, the brain responds by increasing production of a hormone called *melatonin* — a brain chemical that helps you fall asleep, and stay asleep until morning. Levels of melatonin (marketed in pill form to fre-

Opposite page

A slightly modified version of the original, widely-used SPAQ measures the degree of response to the seasonal change to shorter daylight hours. A high score matches the symptoms of SAD. A lower score may suggest the milder feeling of the "winter blues."

Melatonin supplements for jet lag?

For several years now, it has been popular to take melatonin pills to combat the kind of insomnia resulting from time-zone changes. While some studies have shown melatonin supplements to be helpful, others have not. In the favorable experiments, one regimen shown to be effective for traveling eastward is to take melatonin at about 6 PM for three days prior to the flight, and then to continue taking supplements at bedtime for for several days after arriving in the new time zone.

quent fliers who often have to reset their internal clock to a new time zone) typically rise in the evening, and peak at about 2 to 3 AM.

Another central player in the SAD saga is the pineal (literally "pine cone") gland, a pea-sized structure located deep in the center of the brain. This gland acts as a sort of light meter for the brain and body, receiving information from the eyes and producing the melatonin hormone in response to that information. By producing and sending out higher or lower levels of melatonin according to the amount of light the eyes receive, the pineal gland sets and regulates the brain's internal clock.

Many animals besides humans produce melatonin. Squirrels produce extra amounts as the summer solstice passes and the days begin to shorten. For them, high levels of melatonin trigger their food-hoarding behavior, prodding their nut-gathering activities into high gear. For most furry mammals, a seasonal melatonin surge also causes a thickening of the fur in preparation for the cold winter months.

With the approach of winter and the corresponding increase in melatonin levels, humans will also exhibit "hibernation"-type responses, such as eating more food, putting on weight, and sleeping longer hours. However, when the psychological symptoms become too extreme and develop into severe depression, they can seriously interfere with an individual's day-to-day functioning and overall health.

One of the remarkable things about SAD is that women have it more than men by a ratio of about four to one. And younger people suffer from SAD much more frequently than the elderly. The gender difference may result from a greater sensitivity of a woman's pineal gland to changes in daylight hours, while men's brains are apparently tricked by artificial light into thinking that summer never ends. In order to experience the hormonal fluctuation that women do, men must be isolated from the yellow glow of electric bulbs and the shifting blue light of the television set.

Moreover, some population groups appear to have some kind of genetic protection against SAD. A recent Icelandic study turned up very little evidence of winter depression in that country — despite its extreme northern latitude and short winter days.

How not to be SAD

Many experiments have shown that light therapy — daily exposure to intense artificial light emitted by a "light box" — works well to alleviate winter depression in most people. The beneficial effect of light therapy doesn't derive from the kind of ultraviolet radiation emitted by the sun, but rather from sheer brightness. The standard well-lit home or office provides about 300 to 600 lux (with one lux about equivalent to the brightness of a single candle), while a light box offers about 10,000 lux — less bright than the 100,000 lux provided by a sunny summer day, but still enough to alleviate symptoms of SAD. The therapeutic effect of bright light works through the eyes, not the skin. In experiments, people who are naked but blindfolded show no beneficial response to light therapy, while people wrapped like mummies

Fighting east-bound jet lag

Anecdotal accounts from airline flight attendants suggest the following melatonin-free strategy for coping with jet lag on east-bound flights:

Take a nap as soon as possible after arrival, but before the local dinnertime. Do not sleep more than one hour. Rise, shower, dress as if in the morning. Then move into the local time pattern from there on through the remainder of your stay.

A checklist of SAD's symptoms

Do you crave sweets (often chocolate) and starchy foods?

Are you putting on weight?

Do you have less energy?

Are you sleeping more? (*hypersomnia*)

Do you have trouble concentrating?

Do others sense that you are irritable?

In social situations, are you uncomfortable and react more sensitively than usual?

except for their eyes respond well. Light box therapy has to be maintained for an hour or so every day during the entire winter season; otherwise a relapse is all but inevitable.

Antidepressants such as Prozac and Zoloft alleviate the sadness of severe winter blues. These are SSRI (serotonin-increasing) drugs that work by raising brain levels of the transmitter serotonin, the very chemical that the pineal gland converts into melatonin. This interaction seems to be a paradox. For some reason, while high serotonin levels have an *anti*depressant effect, for most people high melatonin levels appear to *cause* depression despite the fact that melatonin is created by the release of serotonin in the brain.

One issue that also needs to be investigated is whether or not SAD is a modern phenomenon resulting from the combination of an ancient brain response to shorter daylight hours with the more complex demands of modern life. If left to follow their internal adjustments to seasonal rhythms, it is quite possible that almost everyone would fall quite naturally into an appropriate winter pattern of long nightly slumbers and reasonable weight gain. In our modern world, however, SAD sufferers must force their bodies to adhere to what is in effect a year-round summer pattern of long days and short nights.

Guide to interpreting SPAQ scores

The questionnaire on page 104 measures the degree to which the individual feels the effects of seasonal change ranging from severe SAD to mild "winter blues." Scores that qualify as these conditions are not a medical diagnosis. They are only indications of the need to consult a doctor.

Question 1. The time of year that mood changes
Winter: If you feel worse in Dec., Jan., Feb. (most common in Western countries).
Summer: If you feel worse in July and August (most common in the Far East).
Winter/Summer: If you feel worse in all those months, enjoying only Spring and Fall seasons.

Question 2. Severity of mood change
The total score range is 24 (most severe) to 0.
4-7 is the average score of unaffected individuals.
8-11 is the winter blues but not symptomatic of SAD.
11 or higher is in the range diagnosed as SAD.
Note that scores will change with north/south moves.

Question 3. Effect on behavior and lifestyle
A score on #2 above of 8 or 9 qualifies as at least a mild case of winter blues
SAD diagnosis applies if problems A-F are all at least "moderate" and the score on #2 above is above 10.
Diagnosis of both winter blues and SAD applies only to individuals who feel symptoms in the winter months.

Questions 4,5,6. Weight gain, sleep, and food choice
None of these are included in a total score. However the answers are taken into account by trained diagnosticians. Studies of hours of sleep report that an average increase of 2.5 hours correlates with SAD and 1.7 hours with the winter blues. Normal increase in winter sleep-time in the northeastern U.S. is 0.7 hours.

WHERE TO LEARN MORE:

Andres Magnusson et al. (2000). "Lack of seasonal mood change in the Icelandic population: results of a cross-sectional study." American Journal of Psychiatry 157: 234-8.

Alexander Neumeister et al. (1999). "Monoamine depletion in non-pharmacological treatments for depression." Tryptophan, Serotonin, and Melatonin: Basic Aspects and Applications, 29-33. New York: Plenum.

Debra J. Skene, Steven W. Lockley, and Josephine Arendt (1999). "Use of melatonin in the treatment of phase shift and sleep disorders." Tryptophan, Serotonin, and Melatonin: Basic Aspects and Applications, 79-84. New York: Plenum.

Robert L. Spitzer et al. (1999). "Jet lag: clinical features, validation of a new syndrome-specific scale, and lack of response to randomized, double-blind trial." American Journal of Psychiatry 156: 1392-1396.

SYNESTHESIA
When the Notes Turn Blue

Diagnosing Synesthesia

Many people have associations between certain sounds or smells and colors — certain musical tones remind them of the color blue, for example. Synesthesia researcher Richard E. Cytowic proposes the following five diagnostic criteria for distinguishing true synesthesia from common, run-of-the-mill sense-blends.

1. **Involuntary:**
   Synesthetes cannot control their cross-sensory experiences.

2. **Projected:**
   The triggered sense is perceived outside the mind, close to the face or body, not simply "in the mind's eye" (or "ear," etc.).

3. **Durable and Unique:**
   True synesthetes always have the same sensory association with any given trigger: if a given word or tone evokes lime-green on one day, for example, it will always do so for the rest of the synesthete's life.

4. **Memorable:**
   The triggered sensory experience is vividly remembered, even if the trigger is forgotten.

5. **Emotional:**
   Synesthetes have an overwhelming, emotional conviction of the reality of their cross-sensory perceptions.

THE BRAIN BASIS OF SYNESTHESIA

How can you taste a color, or see the sound of the letter "M" as a fold of pink flannel? We all know what it means to talk about a bright sound, a dull flavor, or a sharp smell. We might even have some idea what it might mean if a poet described a flavor as "smooth green glass." Now, imagine that every time you tasted a peppermint, you saw columns of green glass so vividly you could virtually reach out and touch them. The difference between someone with *synesthesia* and the rest of us is that "green-glass flavor" is a metaphor for us, but for a synesthete it could be overwhelmingly literal.

Taken all together, the list of conditions on the facing page define the presence of this unusually "talented" abnormality. Literally, synesthesia means a blending of different senses, such that one sense (say, hearing) will trigger a vivid perception in another (say, a color). Someone diagnosed as having this slight brain abnormality that causes this special ability is called a *synesthete*. About ten people in a million are believed to have true synesthesia — although this may be an underestimate, since synesthetes learn to hide their gift from others, lest they be judged insane or at least a little odd. Though their numbers are few, their impact on culture is disproportionately memorable. Not surprisingly, some well-known synesthetes have been artists: the writer Vladimir Nabokov, the artist Vasily Kandinsky, the composer Nikolay Rimsky-Korsakoff, and (most researchers think) the French poet Arthur Rimbaud are a few examples from Western culture.

Nabokov's Letters

Russian-turned-American writer Vladimir Nabokov had vivid visual associations with the letters of the alphabet. These are his descriptions, from his 1949 *New Yorker* article, of the colors he associated with letters of the English-language version of the Latin alphabet:

A = weathered wood

B = burnt sienna

C = light blue

D = creamy yellow

E = yellow

F = alder leaf

G = black vulcanized rubber

H = a drab shoelace

I = yellow

J = pale brown

K = huckleberry

L = a white, limp noodle

M = a fold of pink flannel

N = oatmeal

O = an ivory-backed hand mirror

P = an unripe green apple

Q = "browner than *K*"

R = a sooty rag

S = mother of pearl

T = pistachio-green

U = brassy with an olive sheen

V = rose quartz

W = dull green/violet

X = steely blue

Y = bright gold

Z = blue ink

The idiosyncratic synesthesia of Nabokov

Nabokov's synesthesia primarily involved a kind of colored hearing. Thus, for example, the letter-sound *V* evoked rose quartz, *S* was the color of mother of pearl, and *T* was pistachio-green. It was not just the visual shape of the letter that related to colored images, but the shape along with its sound — such that English *A* conjured up images of weathered wood, while French *A* evoked polished ebony. Only speech sounds triggered synesthetic images for Nabokov; music (which he felt to be "an arbitrary succession of more or less unpleasant sounds") evoked no colors at all.

Rimbaud's Vowels

French poet Arthur Rimbaud was probably a synesthete. His poem *Voyelles* (*The Vowels*), written in 1871, includes these descriptions:

A = black/ a hairy
    corset of black flies
E = white/ lofty glaciers, white kings
I = red/ purple red spittle, laughter of sweet lips
U = green/ green seas, pastures
O = blue

For him, as for many synesthetes, this brain abnormality seemed to run in the family. His mother also had vivid color associations with letters of the alphabet, although only some of her pairings matched his. Perhaps it should not be surprising that the sensory associations are different for each individual with this condition. No two of them share, for example, the same sound-color matchings, although for each person any given pairing is consistent from one day, or year, to the next. For the poet, Rimbaud, the vowel sound "O" was always blue.

"Colored hearing" is the most common form that synesthesia takes.

Hearing sounds, including words, in vivid colors is the most common cross-sensory connection. Taste sometimes, but only rarely, triggers synesthesia in any other sense. And, oddly, while sight can trigger smell, no synesthete has yet been found for whom smell triggers sight.

An aid to photographic memory

Individuals diagnosed as having synesthesia often also have phenomenal recall — sometimes even a photographic memory. Nabokov was known for his prodigious memory. The mnemonic genius named S.V. Shereshevskii — a name known worldwide among cognitive scientists — was characterized by the neurologist A.R. Luria as having "one of the keenest [memories] the literature on the subject has ever described." In fact, his access to such a huge store of data from the past often confused and annoyed him so much he had to devise elaborate procedures to *forget* useless stores of memories. One trick he tried was to write down long lists of numbers he had memorized and then burn the paper he had written them on.

Shereshevskii had a much richer sense of visual hearing than Nabokov: any sound, including not just speech sounds but music, sneezes, and coughs, would trigger vivid images of light and color and, sometimes, sensations of touch and taste as well. Even the characteristic sound of someone's voice would conjure up images; he described one of the psychologists studying him, for example, as having a "crumbly, yellow voice."

One of the reasons Shereshevskii was able to repeat, verbatim, conversations he'd taken part in decades before is that he had stored a wide array of sensory responses to the words he had heard. His memory of the sound of the words would be augmented by sensations of color, light, and sometimes taste, weight, and texture, to form an exceptionally rich and memorable multisensory experience. If he later attempted to recollect what somebody had said on a given occasion days or even decades in the past, he would immediately catch a mistake of even a single word as he "played back" the dialogue because that word did not evoke for him the image, taste, or texture present in his mind during the original conversation.

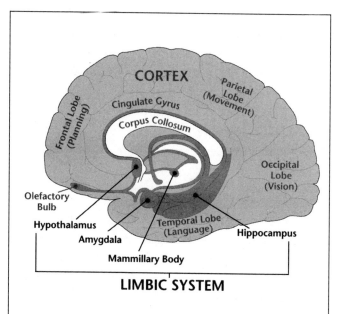

The diagram, left, of the brain's interior shows the "gray matter" of the cortex atop the more primitive limbic system which controls mostly unconsciously, instinctive responses, emotions and memory.

What's happening in the brain of a synesthete: underactive "thinking" centers, and heightened emotional regions

Until very recently, the brain basis of synesthesia was a matter of pure speculation, and the claims of synesthetes were often dismissed as lies or psychosis. New research not only proves the reality of synesthesia, but identifies the brain structures underlying it.

In the brain of a synesthete studied by a leading neurologist, blood-flow brain scans made during an active synesthetic experience revealed a reduction in the flow of blood in the left cortex, indicating that the neurons there were not active. At the same time, blood flow to the subject's limbic system beneath the cortex showed strong activity.

The cortex is the recently-evolved "thinking cap" of the human brain, accounting for most of the thoughts that reach our consciousness. The limbic system is our brain's emotional center, and evolved before the cortex did. When our cortex is suppressed (for example, when we drink alcohol), the impulses of our limbic system become more liberated and rise into consciousness. (Stimulants such as caffeine and nicotine, by contrast, cause neurons in the cortex to fire more actively, but usually only for a short period.)

Have you noticed a little synesthesia in yourself?

One intriguing implication of current brain-scan research findings is that we may all be synesthetes — only we don't know it. Limbic brain structures such as the hippocampus, through which all sensory input passes, are blending color and sound, taste and texture, and light and smell all the time. Recent research indicates that synesthesia is actually a normal brain function in all of us, but its workings reach conscious awareness in only a handful. By this theory, then, it is the activity of our cortex — the most highly human part of our brain which is constantly analyzing new data and comparing it with past experience, looking for patterns — that normally masks these sense-blends from our awareness. If blends of different senses are always taking place in our limbic system, perhaps that's why metaphors such as "bright sound" or "sharp smell" make sense to all of us.

This account would explain why it is, with synesthetes like Shereshevskii, that the sensory associations have little or nothing to do with the meaning of the words — the cortex's domain. Rather, the triggered associations are visceral, often emotionally charged, and so irrelevant to the words' meaning that they serve to confuse rather than to inform. As Shereshevskii himself put it:

> You know there are people who seem to have many voices, whose voices seem to be an entire composition, a bouquet. The late S.M. Eisenstein had just such a voice: listening to him, it was as though a flame with fibers protruding from it was advancing right toward me. I got so interested in his voice, I couldn't follow what he was saying.

WHERE TO LEARN MORE:

Richard E. Cytowic (1993). The Man Who Tasted Shapes. New York: Putnam.

A.R. Luria (1968). The Mind of a Mnemonist. New York: Basic Books.

A.H. Modell (1997). "The synergy of memory, affects and metaphor." Journal of Analytical Psychology 42/1: 105-17

Vladimir Nabokov (1949). "Portrait of my mother." The New Yorker April 9: 33-37.

Vladimir Nabokov (1966). Speak, Memory: An Autobiography Revisited. New York: Wideview/Perigee.

K. Schiltz et al. (1999). "Neurophysiological aspects of synesthetic experience." Journal of Neuropsychiatry and Clinical Neuroscience 11/1: 58-65.

INDEX

Brainwaves® Books is the publishing arm of The Brainwaves® Center, co-directed by Allen Bragdon and David Gamon Ph.D.. The Center's mission is to distill applicable facts from current research in the neurosciences and make that information available to the public in formats that are clear and appealing.

In the last ten years scanning and other non-invasive technologies have equipped science to uncover more about the working of the human brain than was learned in the prior hundred years. The Brainwaves® Center continually reviews scientific literature to select research findings that show promise for improving performance as a practical matter. Science editors dig deeper into selected research to verify it against other published results in the same area.

When they are satisfied that the research results can be understood and applied in real life to strengthen performance they condense the published reports into non-technical English. They advise the reader whether encouraging results derived from animal studies are yet shown to be applicable to humans — work with lab rodents on reversal of obesity, or Alzheimers vaccines are recent examples.

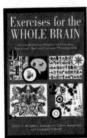

Whenever possible, the editors devise engaging, interactive exercises and tests from research methods and protocols described in the original published reports. These "instruments," often in puzzle formats, activate processing centers that the brain uses to approach real-world problems. The editors also construct self-scoring tests that allow readers to measure their own performance against research norms. Both target varied mixes of cognitive skills involved in applied intelligence.

Can You Pass Any of These 45 Real-Life Professional and Academic Exams?

Recent discoveries about common mental diversities

By translating and publishing selected research results the Center attempts to bring the public up to date on practical ways to improve mental skills—information that, often, only a few research neuroscientists working directly in their narrow areas are yet aware of. The interactive tests, exercises and puzzles entertain and, therefore, engage one or more of the six zones of practical intelligence: Memory, Executive Planning, Effective Social Interaction, Appropriate Emotional Response, Language and Computational Skills, and Constructive Visualization.

Mind-Maintenance Techniques, Tests of Mental Acuity, Exercises for Specific Skills

Left-Brain Conditioning Exercises and Tips to Strengthen Language, Math and Uniquely Human Skills

The books aim to stimulate people's cognitive powers which, especially for an aging population, can help keep life interesting, retard dementia and improve quality of life.